www.pnjhub.com

PNJ Hub

Real estate
Advisory

Paras Mittal
Managing partner
+91 8506916129
+91 9971002715

parascs@gmail.com

About Author

Paras Mittal (ACA,ACS,NCFM)

He is member of Institute of Chartered Accountant and Company Secretary. He is having vast experience in fields of Legal, Tax, Audit, Finance and Corporate Governance of over 14 years.

He dealt in tax audit, internal audit and statutory audit of various large and medium scaled companies.

He consults multinational companies on preparing budget and SOX compliance reports, transfer pricing study and capital commitments reports.

He also handled matters of bank guarantees, STPI approvals, RBI Approvals, CLB and RD Approvals and other license approvals of various statutory authorities.

He served various Multinational companies like Intercontinental Hotels Group, Hilton Hotel Management Services, Chaudhary Group and Galaxy commercial in the past in capacity of Finance and legal head.

His last corporate assignment before venturing into PNJ Group was Head of corporate affairs for Chaudhary Group with USD 3.2 billion dollar turnover.
He was looking over 6 departments with team more than of 50 members across 8 countries and 10 business verticals.

PNJ Professionals network Joint is aggregation platform of professionals into field of merger acquisition, legal dispute, corporate governance, real estate advisory and taxation. This venture is bringing new revolution in service delivery with patent applied process and features like chat with experts, C-suite hiring, E-certification programmes, Office space sharing and Discussion forum. Venture is already live and provide life time business opportunity to freelancers and entrants in professional industry.

His contact details are as follows:

Paras Mittal (ACA,ACS,NCFM)

Legal firm web site: www.pnjlegal.com

Facebook Profile: https://www.facebook.com/paras.mittal.75

Twitter Profile: https://twitter.com/parascs

Linked In Profile: https://www.linkedin.com/in/paras-mittal-1645377 Mb: India +91-8506916129

Disclaimer:

Author and its affiliates do not aims to provide tax, legal, real estate or accounting advice with the help of this book. This material has been prepared for informational purposes only, and is not intended to provide, and should not be relied on for investment, Real estate, tax, legal or accounting advice. This book is compilation of various reference, circulars and notifications and judgments, facts, and recitals on public domain. We reserve rights to allow credits to any particular person or body for the reference taken from his personal viewpoints. You should consult your own Investment, Real estate, tax, legal and accounting advisors before engaging in any transaction.

Table of Contents

I. INTRODUCTION

Real estate is "property consisting of land and the buildings on it, along with its natural resources such as crops, minerals or water; immovable property of this nature; an interest vested in this (also) an item of real property, (more generally) buildings or housing in general Also, the business of real estate i.e. the profession of buying, selling, or renting land, buildings, or housing."

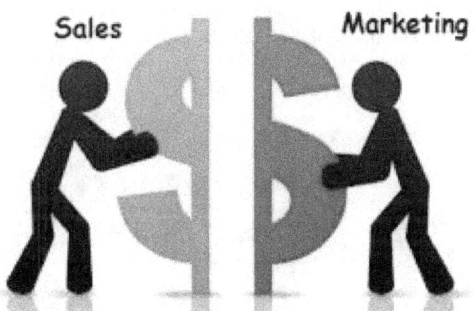

In a country which is rapidly urbanizing and has a severe shortage of housing, owning a piece of real estate is often seen as a prized possession and as means to secure the livelihood of one's family. Even among-st the more privileged classes, real estate ownership holds prominence as either a reflection of social status or as a key investment tool to park excess capital.

However, much in contrast to its importance, the decision to make a real estate purchase is often a consuming process for most individual investors. The problem is compounded in India because of lack of adequate regulation and unavailability of credible information. This has caused many buyers to get stuck in unfortunate situations like delays in project execution, questionable title records or mismatch in promised v/s actual property specifications. Moreover, the lack of adequate financial education means a majority are not aware of optimal financing and taxation benefits.

This is where a professional advisor or advisory firm can add value by assisting clients in making informed decisions. It is however important for a buyer to note the difference between the usual agents who are focused on making commissions and a professional who aims to educate clients by sharing transparent insights. An advisor ensures a hassle free property purchase by providing a differentiated service experience across a number of checkpoints.

II. PLANNING

Real Estate planning is the process of anticipating and arranging, during a person's life, for the management and disposal of that person's estate during the person's life and at and after death, while minimizing gift, estate, generation skipping transfer, and income tax.Estate planning includes planning for incapacity as well as a process of reducing or eliminating uncertainties over the administration of a probate and maximizing the value of the estate by reducing taxes and other expenses. The ultimate goal of estate planning can be determined by the specific goals of the client, and may be as simple or complex as the client's needs dictate. Guardians are often designated for minor children and beneficiaries in incapacity.

The law of estate planning overlaps to some degree with elder law, which additionally includes other provisions such as long-term care

II.1 Things Every Real Estate Investor Should Know To Succeed

In the real estate market, only pro real estate investors understand certain things. They are skilled enough to understand the market really well. They are well aware of the best localities, the history of such places and price trends. As they invest their money in the market they have to understand how real estate markets work, all the way down to the fundamentals. They have to know it all.

In a fast moving market, staying ahead of the competition is the key to becoming successful. To be a pro real estate investor, you need to acquire certain skills and knowledge. This doesn't come easily.

Here are six things that every real estate investor should know.

i. Be systematic

You need to be very well-organised to succeed as a real estate investor. Before starting up your business, you should chart out your strategy very clearly. No matter how big your team is, it is important to build a system. It is easier to get new clients and stay profitable if you are more systematic.

ii. Be aware of price trends

You should have a good idea of current market price trends. Pay attention to how the price of your property compare to other properties in the same neighbourhood and in other localities. Try to understand the market demand and price system really well. They are many good sources of information for buyers and sellers.

iii. Spot new developments

Be aware of all the emerging real estate destinations. Pay attention whenever new roads, multispecialty hospitals, schools, and community centres are being developed. These are signs that an area is growing. On any day, investing in a growing area is more profitable. Studying more about developing area is totally worth your time. Always look for things that homebuyers find attractive. The opening of a new shopping mall or a good school can attract buyers.

iv. Look for low-tax possibilities

Real estate professionals can tell you which all places have the best and worst tax structure. For instance, if there are two equally good localities, it makes sense to buy property in areas which a more favorable property tax structure. Professionals should also be watchful of the reassessment of a place, because it may mean that property taxes are about to rise.

v. Be customer friendly

Always remember that regardless of the effort of you put in, it is the customers who decide whether a property is valuable or not. They are the ones who pay you. Be interactive and answer all possible queries. Customers need to feel satisfied. Reach out and ask people what they want. Learn all the tactics of negotiating.

vi. Be watchful of the peripheries

Real estate in any big city that had started becoming more expensive opens better prospective for other periphery areas. The areas which are adjacent to cities are most likely to be in good demand. Close proximity to railway stations or inter-state bus terminus can make locations highly in demand. Developing new bus routes and roads connecting to major junctions will raise the value of real estate assets.

II.2Periodic Tenancy or Estate for Period to Period in Real Estate

When no specific ending date for a lease is defined, but there is an agreed-upon term, such as month-to-month for occupancy, this is known as a periodic tenancy or estate from period to period. In real estate, this is one type of leasehold estate

The owner or landlord and tenant agree to certain rights and obligations for these periods but do not specify an ending date, so it's an indefinite period of tenancy. Since no ending date is specified, notice per the agreement must be given for termination and vacancy.

A **periodic** tenancy is an **agreement** that runs for an indefinite length of time; there is no set finishing date.
A **periodic** tenancy can be written or verbal. **Rent** may be payable weekly, fortnightly, monthly or any other period agreed by you and the owner.

While generations of Americans have striven to own their homes, there are still millions of single family, condominium, and apartment rental homes. There always will be millions of rental homes because not everyone wants to own or can for various reasons own a home.

Especially after the housing and mortgage market crash, rental homes are in big demand and the cost of renting has been steadily rising.

A **periodic** agreement has a commencement date with no expiry date. The preferred type of **tenancy** is a **fixed-term** agreement where a **tenant** will enter into a 6 or 12- month agreement to give both parties security of **tenancy** and income for a set**period** of time.

Month-to month tenancy is categorized as a periodic **tenancy** in which the **tenant**rents from the property owner one **month** at a time. In the absence of a written or verbal agreement, **tenancy** is considered to be **month to month**.

Fixed-Term **Leases**. A fixed-term **lease** is a type of **rental agreement** in which the renter agrees to stay and pay rent for the period of time indicated in the written**contract**. Renters who break their **lease** typically lose their deposit and, if applicable, their pre-paid rent for the final **month** of the **lease**.

II.3 Succession and estate planning

At a time when many baby-boomers are planning their retirement, the preservation and eventual transfer of your family assets are becoming a major concern. Estate planning aims to minimize the income tax consequences of meeting these objectives.

You will likely own capital property at the time of your death and, in most cases, there will be a tax liability associated with this property. Although you want your estate to be transferred in accordance with your wishes, you also want to pay as little income tax as possible. Therefore, planning has to be done during your lifetime. The main steps in the process include

- financial planning;

- estate freeze;

- life insurance;

- shareholders' agreement, if any;

- powers of attorney in the event of incapacity;

- planned charitable giving, and

- will planning.

A. Succession planning

Survival of a business will depend on the development and implementation of a succession plan. This involves the consideration of a number of issues:

- Continuation of the business

- Development of children's talents

- Preparation of succession

- Choice of successor

- Transfer of ownership, leadership and control of the business

- Adequate retirement income

- Reduction of income taxes The family business brings together a number of players, including shareholders, family members and employees. The

If you can determine your objectives in advance and start the succession process early, you have a better chance of succeeding.

B.Estate freeze/refreeze

You are deemed to dispose of all of your capital property at FMV immediately prior to death. This can produce a significant income tax liability in the year of death.

While this deemed disposition can be deferred when assets are left to a spouse or a spousal trust, this is only a temporary solution to the problem and doesn't solve the issue of eventual transfer to your children.

An estate freeze is a popular method of limiting death taxes. It consists primarily of transferring to a younger generation the growth potential of assets such as real estate or shares of corporations. By doing so, the asset value to the transferor is frozen at its value at the date of transfer.

Accordingly, the amount of potential capital gain on death is also frozen. This will allow you to estimate your potential tax liability on death and better plan for the payment of income taxes.

You can usually accomplish an estate freeze through a transfer of assets to a corporation or an internal reorganization of capital. The mechanics can vary, but the transfer must be professionally planned to avoid the many punitive provisions of the Income Tax Act.

If you have already undertaken an estate freeze, you should consider if now is the time to do a refreeze.

When new shareholders are brought in as part of an estate freeze, a shareholders' agreement should be prepared. At the minimum, this agreement should ensure that there are provisions for the disposal of the company's shares, either by means of a purchase, redemption or transfer. The financing for such transactions should also be considered.

C.Life insurance

Life insurance is a fundamental estate planning tool. If your estate has enough liquid assets, the payment of income taxes may not be much of a problem. But if a major portion of your estate consists of shares of private companies or real estate, it may not be possible to satisfy your tax bill on death without selling off the assets.

Funding potential income taxes through the purchase of life insurance can be an effective estate-planning tool. If sufficient insurance proceeds are available and the policies are properly structured, any income tax arising on the deemed dispositions of assets on your death can be paid without resorting to the sale of your assets.

As insurance needs are constantly evolving, it's important to review your coverage on a regular basis.

As a cautionary note, the government is always looking at ways to close "loopholes" and has recently put a stop to certain more aggressive planning strategies using life insurance. As changes can be announced at any time, it's best to consult with your tax adviser before getting involved with any planning arrangement involving life insurance.

Tax tip: If you decide to acquire life insurance to fund any income taxes owing on the deemed disposition of your private company shares, plan carefully to determine whether you or your company should own the policy. Both options have different advantages. Consultation with your tax and insurance adviser is a must.

D.Asset transfers

If you have decided that you have more assets than you need, you can reduce your estate probate and executor fees, and possibly income taxes upon death, if you transfer assets during your lifetime. If these assets have increased in value since acquisition, however, the transfer could cause an income tax liability.

You should carefully assess which assets to transfer, to whom, and how to avoid triggering a tax liability. Complicated rules apply to income and capital gains on gifts to spouses or common-law partners and children under 18.

E.Planned giving

The value of your estate—and, as a consequence, income taxes and estate administration fees—can be reduced by making charitable donations during your lifetime. The added benefit is that you also earn income tax credits during your life rather than on your death. Other benefits may include the reduction of probate fees and other estate costs.

Planned giving can take many forms. It can involve gifts of life insurance or the establishment of a private foundation, or can be as simple as reviewing your charitable objectives with a view to accelerating your intended donations now to maximize tax savings.

Since many of the planned-giving strategies involve the disposition of capital, you may also have to report income or a capital gain as the result of making a gift. As the name suggests, planned giving consists of planning and giving. "Planning" refers to a careful consideration of estate planning, financial planning and tax planning as part of making the gift. Your tax adviser can help you develop a planned-giving strategy that is most appropriate to your individual situation.

F.Will planning

Both you and your spouse or common-law partner should have wills. This is probably one of the most critical elements of your estate-planning strategy, as dying intestate (without a will) can defeat almost all the estate-planning arrangements you have put into place.

If you die intestate, your assets will be distributed to your spouse, children and parents in accordance with the laws of the province where you resided. This may produce quite different results from what you would have wanted.

An up-to-date will sets down the parameters of your estate plan, indicating in particular the manner in which assets are to be distributed to your heirs and ensures that your wishes are respected. A will also makes it possible to minimize the taxes payable by your estate and your beneficiaries through the use of various provisions in the tax legislation such as testamentary trusts.

Since amendments to the tax laws and changes in your personal situation might change your objectives, your will should be reviewed on a periodic basis.

III. MARKET ANALYSIS

How BIG IS THIS OPPORTUNITY?
MARKET OPPORTUNITY/ANALYSIS

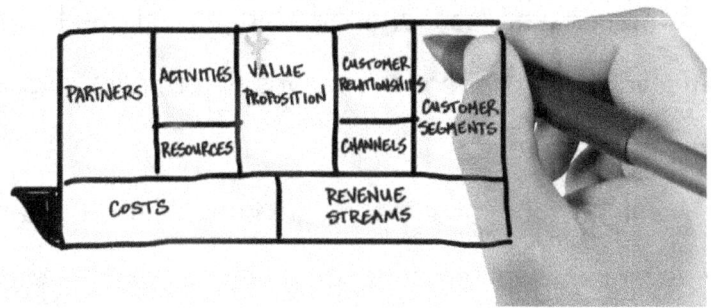

The real estate market has an important bearing on macroeconomic developments and financial stability. Systematic monitoring of real estate market developments and prospects are therefore very important for both a comprehensive analysis of the macroeconomic conditions and prospects of the Greek economy and the effective exercise of the Bank of Greece's supervisory tasks. To this end, the Bank of Greece compiles Real Estate Price Indices by using primary data/estimates about values and quality features of both residential and commercial properties.

III.1 Ways In Which Technology Is Influencing Global Real Estate

Hyper connectivity or rapid globalization has led to a boom of information, services, and knowledge. With the technology affecting every sphere of our lives, information available to real estate investors too is more precise than ever before. As a result of this, global real estate investment is notably high level and is expected to touch giddy heights in the years to come.

Apart from creating an extensive portfolio for investors varying across geographies, investors are using this glut of information to take a well-informed investment decision.

Following are the five technologies that are changing the face of the global real estate.

A. Big data

Technology has changed the way we used gather, store and evaluate information. Whatever data was untrackable before, can be tracked at the click of a mouse. Thanks to the latest technology boom – 'big data' invention. The big-data revolution has transformed our evaluation of urbanization.

B. E-commerce

E-commerce has global acceptance as virtual sellers dominate businesses. For e-commerce, real estate is the key. E-retailers want to be closer to the city, town or suburb so that their products get actively distributed to ensure cost-effective delivery of goods. Small industrial facilities located near urban areas are extremely sought-after due to their location. This will support the supply-chain for e-commerce retailers.

C. Autonomous vehicles

Self-driving cars or automated vehicles are dynamically overshadowing the traditional automobile operation. The advent of automated vehicles will further influence the location of distribution centers near urban areas or city Centre.

The upcoming real estate will need fewer dedicated parking slots as self-driven cars or autonomous vehicles will tackle parking issues. Although this technology is understated and subtle, it has the potential to change the dynamics of commercial and industrial real estate. It will also affect the distribution, supply lines and vehicle accessibility across several industries

D. 3D technology

3D technology has taken the real estate industry by storm. The digital mechanism allows home buyers to not only see the real estate, but also feel the space. From any site or place, people can have a walkthroughs of the property on online portals. Real estate developers are thoroughly using 3D technology to design high quality walkthroughs for the potential homebuyers. Certainly, the 3D technology will move real estate listings much faster.

E. Automation

Home automation is an integral part of the smart home concept. It is the latest technology which will change the way how commercial and residential properties will be used. Through this technology, people can regulate their electricals, appliances and security system at the click of a button. The real estate developers are adapting this kind of technology to offer a contemporary lifestyle to their customers.

III.2 How To Perform Legal Estate Analysis?

A real estate market analysis for an investment property follows the same principles as for a residential property. Basically, you will need to gather data on properties in your area comparable to your property that are currently listed for selling or have been recently sold.

1. The first step is **property analysis**. You have to analyze your property including a wide range of objective and subjective characteristics such as:

   - Area and neighbourhood

   - Size or square footage

   - Land area

   - Number of bedrooms and bathrooms

   - Other rooms

   - Number of floors

   - Construction age

   - Amenities and features such as swimming pool, garden, fireplace, balcony, veranda, etc.

- Location with respect to roads, marketplaces, public transportation, schools, etc.

- Recent improvement

2. The next step is to **identify a few recently sold properties** in your area that are comparable to yours. We recommend looking at past listings within a radius of 1 to 3 miles from your property. Start with homes that were sold within the past 3 months and, if needed, extend to 6 months. For your comparative market analysis, aim to find a few (we recommend 3-5) comparables – or comps – i.e., properties that are similar to yours in terms of size, age, location, and other features.

3. Then **look for current listings of comparable homes.** Again, focus on a distance of 1-3 miles away from your property and identify at least 3 homes that are comparable to yours. Be careful. When it comes to active listings, keep in mind that listed prices are prospective, not necessarily real values. Many sellers tend to have high expectations and list their homes for a much higher price than their actual value. The value of unsold homes is highly affected by real estate

trends. Generally the sellers' market attempts to inflate values, while the buyers' market attempts to deflate them. Thus, you should use active listings only as a supplement to recently sold properties' values.

4. You should also **consider pending listings** – these are recently finalized deals which have not been fully closed yet. In your real estate market analysis, analyzing pending listings will give you a good idea about how the real estate market is doing at this very moment.

5. **Look at expired listings.** These will be of indispensible help in your comparable market analysis. Usually the reason for listings to expire is that the price was too high. If there are listings for homes comparable to yours that have expired, you should probably not ask for a price as high as theirs.

6. Once you have gathered the needed info, you should choose one property – from the 3-5 comps that you have found – which is definitely worth more than yours. Maybe it is in a better location (off a noisy street, close to a bus stop, or next to a park), offers

better amenities (a nice view), or is a newer construction. Set this as your **ceiling value**.

7. Then select one property that is for sure worth less than yours. This will be the **floor price**.

8. Now you have a **price range**, and your property market value should fall somewhere within this range. The next step is to **compare your property** to the ones that you have selected. Consider the size, the age, the amenities, upgrades and renovations, subjective features, and the location. Check out the exterior of the sold homes and the neighbourhoods in which they are located.

9. Finally, you have to decide where your property falls within the selling price range of the comps that you have chosen. **This is the market value of your home.**

Conducting a real estate market analysis on your own is an intimidating task. However, it is doable and will give you a good insight into the valuation process. To conclude, one simple piece of advice – don't fall into the trap that has caught many sellers, namely overpricing. While you want to make sure that you don't sell your property for less than what it is worth, you also don't want to massively overprice at the beginning. This will force you to eventually bring down the price when your property has lost its freshness on the market.

III.3 What Does Estate for Years, Mean in Real Estate?

Definition: In real estate, one type of leasehold estate is the estate for years, or estate for term.

In this type of lease, there is a defined specific beginning date and an ending date for a specific term. This means that no notice to vacate is required, as the ending date of the lease is when the tenant should vacate the property.

The lease cannot be terminated before expiration unless both parties agree. The rights and obligations of the owner or landlord and the tenant are spelled out in the lease.

Also Known As: estate for term

Seven Common Clauses from Leases

1. Joint and Several Liability

Used a lot in residential leases, this clause allows the landlord to treat multiple tenants as each being individually and jointly liable to uphold the terms of the lease. In other words, the group is responsible, but so is each individual. If there are six roommates sharing the rent and on the lease, the landlord need only serve one or more to meet lease terms for notice.

2. Default

There needs to be a clause setting out what happens if either party to the lease defaults on the terms. It should also state when a party is considered in default. It's OK just to state that a default occurs when one party violates the terms of the lease, but it's better practice to list the ways in which an automatic default occurs to make it very clear. It would be a "not limited to" clause, meaning any other terms not listed would still trigger default, if violated.

3. Subleasing

Some leases forbid subleasing. Landlords often say that it's difficult to impossible to enforce, so they allow it. You can charge a fee or increase rent if subleased. It's good practice in this clause to require a complete application process, including credit and background check for sublease tenants.

4. Late Fees

To encourage on-time rent payments, late fees can be charged. Check state laws, however, to determine if specific grace periods are required or other rules related to late rent penalties. Be clear as to when a late fee kicks in and the amount. If this isn't clear in the lease, backing up charging a late fee in court will be tough.

5. Severability

This is an important clause. At times, sometimes because laws change, a portion of a lease can be declared illegal. This clause clearly states that if one portion of a lease is declared illegal, all other portions of the lease will still be legally enforceable.

6. Lease Renewal

There are various ways to handle lease renewal in the agreement. The most common are automatic or non-automatic. If automatic renewal is used, the tenant will be automatically liable for another lease period when the renewal date passes. This puts the onus on the tenant to inform the landlord in advance and terminate the lease.

The more common non-automatic lease renewal will usually require a specific amount of notice if the tenant is not going to renew. If notice isn't received by that date, there is some sort of monetary penalty, as the landlord doesn't have as much time to find a new tenant to reduce the vacancy period. Either way, it is a best practice for the landlord to set up internal alerts so that the tenants can be reminded before any important due dates.

7. Use of the Property

Be careful not to violate laws related to discrimination here. Generally, the one thing to be sure to do is to limit the number of unit occupants. You can leave the number open until you know how many, so if three people move in with your approval, the lease would then limit the occupants to three. This keeps unwanted boyfriends/girlfriends or family members from moving in.

Those are common lease clauses, but you always want to get a lease agreement properly constructed for your state, as laws vary and you want to stay on the right side.

IV.   MARKET CONDITION

Market's condition refers to market's characteristic(s) such as number of the competitors, level or intensity of competitiveness, and the market's growth rate that a firm walks into when introducing a new product.

IV.1 Contingencies in Real Estate Contracts

By definition, a contingency is a provision in a real estate contract that makes the contract null and void if a certain event were to occur. Think of it as an escape clause that can be used under defined circumstances. It's also sometimes known as a condition.

A typical contingency clause might read like this: "This contract is contingent upon Buyer successfully obtaining a mortgage loan at an interest rate of 6 percent or less."

If rates rise suddenly so this rate is longer be available, the contract would end. It would no longer be binding on either the buyer or the seller.

A number of very normal and common contingencies appear in most real estate contracts and transactions.

Mortgage Approval

A contract will typically spell out that the transaction will only be completed if the buyer's mortgage is approved with substantially the same terms and numbers as are stated in the contract. In other words, if the contract specifies a down payment of 30 percent and a conventional 30-year loan, that's what should be approved by the lender. It's generally just a turn-down or approval for those terms, but sometimes a buyer will be offered a different deal and the terms will change.

Insurance Approval

A buyer would not want to close on a home—and the lender definitely would not close on it—if the buyer was unable to get homeowner insurance. The buyer should immediately apply for insurance to meet deadlines for a refund of earnest money if the home can't be insured for some reason. Sometimes past claims for mold or other issues can result in trouble getting affordable homeowner insurance.

Appraisal

The deal should be contingent upon an appraisal for at least the amount of the selling price. Should the appraisal come in lower, another negotiation might become necessary to see if the seller will lower the price to make up the difference. If not, this could void the contract.

Closing Date

The completion of the transaction is typically contingent upon it closing on or before a specified date. Let's say that the buyer's lender has a problem and can't fund the deal by the closing/funding date cited in the contract. Technically, the seller can back out, although the closing date is usually just extended unless the seller has another higher offer waiting in the wings. Then he might want to leave the current deal so he can accept it.

Inspection Related

The deal might be contingent upon the buyer accepting the property "as is." This is common in foreclosure deals where the property may have experienced some wear and tear or neglect. More often, there are various inspection-related contingencies with due dates and requirements that the buyer must accept the inspection results or object to them with terms for repairs. The seller can then either accept or reject those terms.

Satisfactory Walk-Through

The closing will happen if the buyer is satisfied with a final walk-through of the property the day of or the day before closing. There would be problems should a light fixture, door, or included appliance was missing, or the property otherwise suffered some damage since the time the contract was entered into.

The Sale of Another Home

Sometimes the buyer is only able to close if he can get funds from the sale of his current home, which is usually under contract at the time he enters into the deal for the new home. The new deal is contingent upon that deal closing and funding. A seller might not accept the buyer's offer if it includes this contingency if he has others coming in.

Just About Anything

Either the seller or the buyer can propose almost any type of contingency in a contract negotiation, but that doesn't mean it will be accepted. Contingencies are common and normal in real estate transactions. They're usually just part of the process and everything moves along smoothly, but every now and then either the buyer or seller side can cause problems.

IV.2 Flipping in Real Estate: A Quick 'Buy and Sell' Strategy

Flipping in the real estate world means buying low and selling high in the market. Flipping is a type of property investing which focuses on getting quick return on your investment. You buy a property and then sell it for a higher price on the total investment keeping in mind the money spent on buying, renovating and holding the property.

The basic idea to enter into a real estate flip is with the help of making quick money. If you are smart and if done correctly, a flip can provide you with large profits. You should always do your market research before **buying a property**.

Try to figure out the pros and cons before investing. Do a thorough research to know about the demands in that area, browse through the ads to find the deals that suit you. Know the present asking rate and look at the houses that have been recently sold. You buy a property and the next step would be a little bit of renovation.

While putting your property for sale consider the total cost (renovations plus legal hassles) and then quote a higher price so that you gain in the deal. Increase your network by creating new contacts with realtors, attorneys, brokers and other investors. Remain professional during dealings with people. If you are capable of concentrating on challenges as much on benefits and profits, you will come out a winner.

IV.3 Growth of Real estate in India

The Indian real estate market is not very transparent. The Indian real estate market is extremely fragmented, and the public does not have much access to information and data that they do need.

The real estate industry also does not have "industry status". So, markets are very locally oriented, and not as interdependent as they ought to be. This is why Indian real estate markets are very heterogeneous.

However, it is important to study real estate markets and make sense of how consumers, investors, developers and corporate occupiers fit into the overall framework. International property consultants (IPCs) help a lot in understanding the system in depth and detail.

Real estate developers and other stakeholders do well when they adapt to domestic market conditions, while staying attuned to global trends.

While buying, selling and developing property, market research is very important. A consultant who really understands the market can help a lot in taking the right

42

decision. Users and developers alike benefit from the research of property consultants.

The Indian government is also using modern technologies like Geographic Information System (GIS) to recover property taxes and understand real estate markets better. Market research consultants collect and analyze information related to various aspects of property markets. Over years, property consultancy firms are likely to develop a good database that will help them forecast trends more accurately. Consultants will be able to understand market trends across different real estate asset classes more accurately.

A. The growth of real estate market research in India

Till 2005, there was not much data on Indian real estate markets, and developers used to rely on their own judgment. As the markets were not well developed, they did not have much of an option, and this approach was working fine. But after 2005, foreign investment in the sector rose, and more international players entered the market. The expertise they brought in changed the face of Indian real estate markets. Developers can no longer rely on their gut feeling alone. It is risky to go by gut feeling in a more sophisticated market.

Developers slowly started employing market research consultants. They also commission market studies to take decisions that are more informed. As far as Indian real estate markets are concerned, these are very recent developments. The market research of international property consultants (IPCs) in India are comparable to that of their counterparts elsewhere.

B. The growing significance of consultants

Indian real estate developers and other firms no longer underestimate the importance of expert market research. Private equity (PE) funds have always preferred to get a second opinion from real estate consultants on their entry/exit strategies. PE firms continue to rely on their advice, even after they have taken such key decisions.

Foreign institutional investors (FIIs) and PE funds made international property consultants (IPCs) an important part of the real estate industry, in India and in other parts of the world. It is PE firms and FIIs that made developers see how IPCs have changed the way real estate industry operates. The growth of these funds has played an important role in the process.

C. What is the future of real estate market research?

In the near future, because of the development of real estate markets, the research industry will grow too. Currently, IPCs are playing two important roles. IPCs manage data and provide important data to their customers. IPCs also make expert advisory facilities available.

In the future, when the real estate sector becomes more transparent, and when technology becomes more integrated, the importance of data will lessen. The advisory role of IPCs, however, will start playing a more dominant role.

We live in an age of specialization. We will see the importance of specialization and data analytics in the real estate sector too. This has already happened to a much larger extent in developed markets.

PNJ Hub created new service delievery modelfor Real estate in India

PNJ Hub has launchedthe unique networking hub inIndia. PHJ Hub is an online consultingplatformthatgives access to services in Vastu, InteriorDesigning, Legal Dispute andSettlements, Taxation, CorporateGovernance& Compliances, MergersandAc□uisitionsand Real Estateadvisory. PNJ Hub is driven by the CEO, ParasMittal who is seasoned professional and having vast experience of 12 years.

It   isinterestingto   note thatalargenumberofsearchengineoptimizationcompanies   have added hub creation and promotion as partof their service.

This is primarilyduetothe versatile advantagesthatthisparticular platform hasto offer.

Now creating a hub page isnot rocket science, but a number of timepeople will savebyoutsourcing this task to a reliable outsourcingcompanywill enable themto concentrate on their corebusiness with greater benefits. However, PNJ Hub aspirestobepreferredconnectingplatformforservice seekers and providers acrossand beyond the above-mentionedcategories.

 PNJ Hub willbring about arevolutioninthereal estate service industryinIndiabyimplementingthefollowing   in   real   estate advisory:

- ❖ Custodyof   documents: Service   providers   are boundtokeepclients' documents confidential atalltimesand also hand over theworkingfilesanddocumentstothe PNJ Hub at each milestone.
- ❖ Service restoration: PNJ Hub will give people thechoiceto restore servicesat any time of the collaboration.
- ❖ Continuousfeedback: PNJ Hub willre☐uestregularfeedback from people of India to ensure the utmost☐ualityof service.

- ❖ Regular Payment: PNJ Hub willchargepeopleofIndiaonaregularbasisonthe status ofworkand relieve service providers fromthe tension of tracking ofthe payments.
- ❖ Termination of contract: PNJ Hub gives Service providersthefreedomtodiscontinuetheworkwithremunerat ionforthetaskscompleted.

PNJ Hub isallabout bridging thegapbetweenpeople who needprofessional services, andthose who canprovidethemwith passion andcommitment. By joining PNJ Hub, thepeople of India will have access tothegreatbenefitswhich include: sharing the office space on per hour, technical chat with experts on per 5 min basis, hiring of C suite professionals on per day basis, and also doing E certification programme.

PNJ Hub offersexcellence in providing professional real estate businessservices, give it a trial.

For further information about PNJ Hub, visit www.pnjhub.com

V. DOCUMENTATION

V.1 Document Validation

The validity of an appraisal of real estate property is in jeopardy if changes to the property or its surroundings have a negative effect. A bank may or may not be able to use the appraisal for a subsequent transaction. The Guidelines address supervisory matters relating to real estate appraisals and evaluations used to support real estate transactions, and they provide specific guidance to examiners and regulated institutions about several aspects of an institution's appraisal and evaluation programs, including:

> ➤ Procedures for obtaining an appraisal or evaluation report in a timely manner to facilitate the institution's underwriting decision.
> ➤ Selection criteria and procedures to evaluate and monitor the performance of individuals who perform appraisals and evaluations.
> ➤ Criteria for using an existing appraisal or evaluation to support a subsequent transaction.
> ➤ Internal controls for promoting compliance with the appraisal regulation. This article examines the third item, typically referred to in the appraisal and lending industry as a "validation" analysis.

This procedure is used to determine whether a value estimate presented in a previous appraisal report remains valid. The validation specifically aids in determining if negative changes have occurred to the physical condition of a property or to the marketplace in which it is located. If such changes are found to have occurred since the date of the previous appraisal, then a new appraisal of the property should be recommended.

V.1.A Factors to Consider in Validation

A qualified staff person (that is, licensed staff appraiser or loan officer) within the institution may perform the validation or the institution may enlist the original appraiser or another qualified appraiser to review the original appraisal or evaluation report, inspect the property, and research the marketplace. Regardless of who is chosen, the validation must include a reexamination of relevant market conditions, an analysis of comparable market data, an inspection of the collateral, and a conclusive written opinion regarding the validity of the original report. Institutions may ask the previous appraiser to perform an "update appraisal" to confirm the continued validity of the original value. In any case, the validation must be performed in an unbiased and professional manner acceptable to the agencies governing the institutions, and the regulated institution must properly document the basis for its findings and keep the documentation in the loan and/or credit file.

V.1.B look at the broader picture

Before we dive into the specifics of your local real estate market, a bit of background first. Real estate is one of those industries that is heavily influenced by environmental, political, social, and broader economic forces that affect property value and pricing, as well as people's buying and selling decisions. Additionally, the real estate market is shaped by these four factors:

- **Demand:** This is both the quantity of homes wanted, at a specified price at a specific time, and buyers' willingness and ability to purchase a home (i.e., homes are for sale that a buyer can afford and wants to purchase).
- **Rarity:** This refers to the limited supply of certain types of property in particular locations (i.e., the buyer is ready and able, but a property is not available, so the sale won't take place).
- **Utility:** This factor asks the question: "Is the commodity suitable for use?" (i.e., the buyer might be ready and able, the property might be available, but if the residence is riddled with asbestos, the sale still will not take place until the problem is remedied).
- **Transferability:** This refers to the ability of the home to legally change hands. For example, if all the other

elements line up, but the buyer discovers that the seller's name is not on the title or another legal encumbrance with the deed, he or she still cannot purchase the property.

Also, the following ten core economic principles are at play. If you have a basic knowledge of them, you can help your clients with pricing, purchasing, and selling decisions.

- **Anticipation:** Bases real estate's value on its future profitability and advantages.
- **Balance**: Property attains maximum value when the production agents are economically stable. Productions agents are the necessary components to bring a commodity or service to market: land, labor, capital, and coordination.
- **Change:** Value is influenced by variations both inside and outside of the market.
- **Competition:** The striving between parties to develop, offer, or obtain real estate and the contest between properties to capture consumer attention. Property worth is impacted by both types of competition.
- **Conformity:** Value increases the more similar a property is to others in the same category or location.
- **Contribution:** The feature of a property is only as valuable as it increases its worth.

- **Externalities:** The value of real estate is impacted by "external" conditions such as the four value forces—economic, social, political, and environmental.
- **Highest and best use:** The legal use of a parcel of land, which, when capitalized, will generate the greatest net income.
- **Substitution:** A property's value cannot be greater than the sale price of those with similar features and utility.
- **Supply and demand:** When supply is high, and demand is low, the price of real estate is low; conversely, when supply is low and demand is high, the price is high.

Your local real estate market: what you need to know

Now that you have an overview of the factors that affect the overall real estate industry let's dig in and take a closer look at understanding your real estate market on a local level. Start by collecting this data:

- Your company's market share and penetration
- The performance of competitors in your local market
- Real estate services that are in demand
- Listing and sales data—such as average volume sold, property prices, and appreciation rates

- Features of listed and recently sold properties
- Financing data
- Demographics (population data)
- Other economic, social, political, and environmental data as it impacts your unique area

Your broker, real estate board, firm's multiple listing service (MLS), or a professional real estate organization can help you track down that information. You can also turn to these sources for additional data or to fill in any gaps:

- Banks and credit unions
- Federal Reserve System
- Builder associations
- Key local employers
- Bureau of Labor Statistics
- Local building department
- Business review journals
- Mortgage brokers and bankers
- Census Bureau
- Municipal planning commission
- Chamber of Commerce
- School district
- County office
- Tax appraiser's office
- Data service organizations

- Title companies
- Electric company
- Water company
- Visitor's bureau
- Employment agency
- Wall Street Journal
- Federal Home Loan Bank Board

The payoffs of understanding your real estate market

While it can seem like a great deal of work to track down and study all of that information, the payoffs are tremendous. For example, you can:

- **Use the data to evaluate your performance.** With all that data, you can quickly see how many agents you are competing with, their experience levels, and how you rank against other agents in your brokerage and in your area. Plus, you gain insight that will allow you to set financial goals and other objectives.
- **Fully understand market conditions.** You will know what's fueling or stalling the market, and whether you are dealing with a buyers' or sellers' market. That allows you to keep in check both your and your clients' expectations as they seek to buy or sell a property.

- **Offer clients better advice.** Understanding your real estate market allows you to establish and evaluate the price of a listed property and help your seller and buyer clients make the right decisions. Those two things are key to growing your real estate business.

- **Position your clients' properties against competing real estate.** The data helps you determine what buyers should offer in order to get a fair deal or how sellers should price a property. You can gain insight, specifically from your MLS, about how old the average listing is, what percentage of listings actually sell, how listing prices compare to sale prices, what are the most active segments of the local market, and what are the features of the properties that are currently listed or have recently sold.

- **Create promotional opportunities.** You can build your credibility and land new clients by sharing your economic know-how during phone and in-person conversations with prospects and when you connect with past clients or ask for referrals. Additionally, you can share your knowledge via blog, social media, newsletter, or the media, to build your reputation as a thought leader. That increases people's trust in you as an expert.

- So many agents don't take the time to know their market. When you put time and effort into fully understanding your real estate market, you immediately gain a competitive advantage. The more you know, the better you can serve your clients and guide them toward making the best decisions. When you provide outstanding service to clients, they will not only keep you on as their agent, but also refer you to other clients. And that is how you succeed in this business.

V.2 Legal documents you need to buy property

Property buying can often be messy. Jargons float around and you can be confused with all the legalese. We made it simple for you. Use this handy guide to help you navigate the real estate pitfalls you may encounter while buying a home. While purchasing property, it is essential to check that the following documents are in order:

1) Agreement to sell

It is the first document prepared in anticipation of a sale of the property. It contains a detailed description of the property and states the terms of conditions between the buyer and the seller, including the purchase price as agreed upon.

2) Absolute sale deed and title deed

The sale deed or title deed is the most important document that records the actual transfer of ownership of the property. It needs to be registered at the sub registrar's office under whose jurisdiction the property would fall.

3) Title search and report

Property title search is a process of retrieving the chain of documents relating to the history of the property that has been registered with the concerned authority. It includes a description of the property and names of title holders, joint tenancy, etc. It is especially important for procuring a home loan.

4) Khata certificate

This document is known by different names in different states and it provides proof that the property has an entry in the local municipal records.

5) Receipt of property tax

The receipts of property tax hold that the previous owner or occupier had paid all the taxes and none have been left as due. They also establish the legal status of the property and therefore serve as an important document of evidence.

6) Encumbrance certificate

An encumbrance certificate states that the property is free from all encumbrances or loans. It is a key document for procuring a loan against property from banks. It has all the details about transactions relating to the property.

7) Occupancy certificate

An occupancy certificate or completion certificate is given by the municipal corporation after the construction of a building to establish that it was constructed according to a sanctioned plan and that it is ready to be occupied.

8) Statement from bank if loan outstanding

If any loan is outstanding on the property that is being purchased, it is safe to procure the statements relating to the loan so that there is full disclosure in that regard.

9) Non-objection certificates

It is important to ask the developer to produce copies of various NOCs that must be procured from various departments such as the Sewage Board, Pollution Board, Environment Department, Traffic and Coordination Department, etc. This forms the 'intimation of disapproval' for the construction of the building

10) Sanctioned building plan by statutory authority

This is to ensure that the buyers are cautious about any deviations from the sanctioned plan made by the developer.

11) Power of Attorney/s, if any

A Power of Attorney is required in original if any person is acting on the authorization of the owner of the property. It could be general or specific.

V.3The Importance Of Documentation And Sequence Of Execution In Real Estate Transactions

In real estate, documentation is very key. Real estate is the type of asset that is immovable and highly illiquid; in layman's language it means it cannot be sold quickly. It can be there for years and yet remain where it is. You can hardly sell real estate in an hour or a day like other assets.

The processes that come with the sales of real properties is incomparable, which means it is not as liquid as other assets. Hence, the singular fact that real estate is immovable makes documentation very important.

Another characteristic of real estate is its durability; durability in this context means a situation where land cannot be destroyed or put to ruin. Land will always be where it has been from time immemorial, ownership will change from time to time but the land will never cease to exist.

Again, land has existed since creation, only ownership of land has been transferred from time to time or hand to hand. This transfer of ownership can only be validated through documentation.

Documentation is highly pivotal in transactions involving landed properties or real estate as a whole. This brings me to the aspect of sequencing in real estate which is equally as important as documentation; In fact both should come hand in hand.

Let's use rental properties in real estate as a case study. Take for example, when a tenant takes up a property having being satisfied with the price, the contract of agreement, exchange letter among other things, there should be an agreement called tenancy agreement between the landlord and the tenant done by a lawyer.

If this agreement is just dumped and not signed, it will be of no use or benefit. This means that it can't be tendered when it is needed in a court of law.

This implies that every document needs to be executed for it to become tenable, enforceable or for it to become an agreement binding the participants going into the contract.

Therefore, tenancy agreement binds the landlord and the tenant. Refusal to sign tenancy agreement yet gaining possession of a tenanted space may become a huge problem in the future. It will be almost impossible to get that tenant to sign the agreement afterwards especially in this part of the world.

The tenant has gained possession of the property by moving into the house or office he transacted. You may probably be on a lost cause getting him to sign the documents especially when he does not agree with the contents of the letter. The situation gets worse if there are things in the agreement he doesn't agree with and there are issues that were not discussed prior to his occupying the said property.

The implication of this is that the tenant may stay in that property until the expiration of his rent without putting pen to paper. Eventually nothing will seem to bind the tenant and the landlord.

The above premise is enough reason sequence should not be overlooked in transactions involving real estate.

The right sequence should come in this order;

1. There should be a meeting between both parties where your terms of contract is discussed and agreed upon.

Afterwards, a contract document in form of tenancy agreement is drawn out.

2. Both parties should have at least one copy of the agreement before the tenant moves into the property for the period specified.

Now, the essence of this is to forestall any problem that may arise in the immediate future. In a situation where the aforementioned steps are not taken, it then becomes a challenge when the tenant becomes problematic or does not agree with some actions taken by the landlord.

If the contract of agreement is later brought to the notice of the tenant who has already rented the property, the landlord will not be able to force him to sign and subsequently the tenant could hold him to ransom.

Going down memory lane, there was a situation that came up some years back where the estate management team of an estate property and the residents were having a challenge that had to do with services rendered to the residents. The issues bordered around service charge. The leader of the protest carried out by the residents was quoted on the pages of the newspaper to have said that he did not have any agreement with the estate managers, neither did he sign any document yet he's being living in the estate and had now become a source of worry for the estate management team.

That is why the issue of documentation should never be neglected in any real estate transaction. It was earlier buttressed in the course of this article that documents are important, albeit, the sequence of execution of this document is equally important. Please never take it for granted.

V.4 Legal documentation and clearances

Ask for copies of all necessary permissions prior to making any financial commitment. Check the following documents and clearance certificates to avoid getting into any legal tangle in future:

1. Land Record

Title deed is the most important document as it gives details about ownership, rights, obligations and mortgages on the property. So it validates whether the land where the project is coming up has been registered and development rights transferred. Get a copy of it from the builder and cross-check the information with the land record office.

2. Construction Clearances

A 'certificate of commencement' is mandatory to commence any construction.

3. Approved Planning

It is good to run an additional check and verify that the building plan and layout plan has been approved and no byelaw applicable in the area has been broken. Make sure that the floor where you have booked your flat has been approved in the building plan.

The layout should be in accordance with the National Building Code of India (NBC). NBC is a comprehensive guideline, a code, for regulating the building construction activities across the country. Get this document verified with the local municipal authorities.

4. Land Use Certificate

It is illegal to have residential properties on a commercial or industrial zone. Apply to the urban development authority and check the certificate to ensure that the property you plan to purchase is in the residential zone. Sometimes the land will be in what is called a 'converted zone'. Cities are expanding and often agricultural land is converted for non-residential usage by paying a fee to the government. In such a case, check for the endorsement order given by the tehsildar or deputy commissioner of the zone that licenses residential construction on that land.

5. Master Plan of the Area

Often builders claim future infrastructural development of the area such as upcoming metro or highway near the project. Don't believe everything blindly. Look at the area's master planning to verify. These plans are easily available with the town planning department.

6. Ask the Experts

An easy way to verify that the project has clean paperwork is to see if it has loan approvals from financial institutions. Banks have stringent lending rules and do their necessary due diligence before clearing loans. However, this is not always error-free and there have been many cases In the past where the builder had bank support, but the project landed in legal troubles. It is therefore better to get professional help. If necessary get a paid opinion.

V.5 STEPS IN VALIDATION

1. REVIEW OF SITUATION

- A validation should include a thorough review of the original appraisal or evaluation, compilation and analysis of relevant market data on the subject neighborhood and comparable markets, and a formal site inspection of the subject property and the surrounding neighbor63 Validating Previous Appraisals and Evaluations hood.

2. POST REVIEW

- The review should always be the first step. The lender will then understand the quality and condition of the subject and its marketplace at the time of the original transaction. Interviewing the loan officer or asset manager, the property owner, tenants, and local brokers may also provide insight into the property itself and the marketplace.

3. KNOWLEDGE

- Upon gaining sufficient knowledge of the property and its marketplace, market data, such as rental rates, sale prices of similar use properties, and current building costs can be gathered and analyzed to identify obvious trends in market value.

4. INSPECTION

- A thorough site inspection of the subject property and its surrounding neighborhood should then follow to reveal further indication of decline or improvement. If any changes have occurred from the date of the original appraisal or evaluation, they should be documented and included with the collateral or credit files of the institution. Furthermore, in cases where negative changes are found, a new appraisal or evaluation should be recommended to adequately determine the amount of value lost. If there appear to be no changes (the market is stable) or if the changes are positive (property appreciation is evident), a new appraisal or evaluation would not be necessary, and the value in the previous appraisal or evaluation can be recommended as still valid.

A validation is a simple comparison of values at two points in time. It answers the question: Is the value in a previous appraisal or evaluation still valid in the current marketplace? In other words, is the subject's potential current value equal to or greater than the value estimated in the previous appraisal or evaluation?

The two most important factors to consider in a validation are the physical condition of the property itself and the strength of the subject's current real estate marketplace compared to when the previous appraisal was performed. A blanket assumption about the validity of all past values based solely on a current position in the real estate cycle would be inappropriate, as the determination can depend on the particular date of a prior valuation.

A validation of a prior appraisal or evaluation can be a straightforward task when real estate values are increasing across the board, but trends are difficult to assess in the current environment of complex, dynamic real estate markets. For example, some widely respected real estate analysts conclude that the current commercial real estate cycle has peaked, while others assert that it has yet to reach its apex. Evaluating the appropriateness of a validation in such a climate necessitates a property-by-property and market-by-market approach. Changes in values may depend, for example, on the specific property type (such as industrial, office, or retail), fluctuating cycles of development between neighborhoods, supply and demand factors in a submarket, or the economic strength of a metropolitan area. Regardless of the position in the real estate cycle, however, a validation is a reasonable and cost-effective way for institutions to reevaluate the strength of their real estate portfolios.

V.6 Property Documents Verification

Property Document verification helps property-seekers to protect from any property disputes and fraudulence.

Investment in real estate is a big investment. Its gives you great benefits in present as well as in future in the form of investment return. But if you're investing the huge amount of money on real estate properties, then it's mandatory for you to be aware and take each step very carefully. If you want to avoid property disputes and related issues in future, and if you don't want to face any big loss in property dealing, then property documents verification is helpful for you.

Here are major purposes behind Property Documents Verification:

- To evaluate the authenticity of documents issued by property owner and realtors.
- To ensure that the documents are under the legal regulations or not.
- To make sure that property is free from any disputes and issues or not.
- To ensure the approval of local authority.
- Ascertain clearance certificate under Urban Land Ceiling Act, 1976.
- To ensure the authenticity of the realtor and their standard in the market.
- To ascertain the approval of development authorities for the construction projects.
- To make sure that the property site is government approved or not.
- To ascertain all required legal documents and disclosure are full-fledged and genuine.

It's a fine thing to ensure that your property documents are genuine and verified. It helps property owners to be confidence and tension-free towards their property. After all, property is the biggest asset for any person and property documents are the proof of ownership of property.

VI. PROPERTY VALUATION

In real estate, property values are not the same as property prices. Property value is an estimate of what a home or a piece of land is actually worth; the price may be higher or lower, depending on who has the best bargaining skills, who wants the deal most and whether there were any incentives thrown in to sweeten the deal.

VI.1 Why Property Valuation is Important

Property valuation is a key concept in real estate investing. If you don't know the value of an investment property, you won't be able to know how much rent to charge or how much to pay in property taxes. Estimating these two figures, along with others like property insurance, is not possible without knowing a property's value.

So, how do you find out a property's value? The answer is through a home appraisal. A home appraisal is a professional opinion about the value of a real estate asset at a specific point in time. An appraiser is a professional who evaluates a property's value. The value of a rental property is known as its fair market value. Market conditions, location, and a variety of other factors influence fair market value.

Now that we've covered the importance of market value, it's time to discuss the three main property valuation methods:

1.) Sales Comparison Approach

The most popular of the property valuation methods is the sales comparison approach. Also known as the market data or comparable sales approach, this method is mostly used for land and residential real estate, especially single family homes. Valuation in this method is done by comparing a real estate property with similar properties in terms of sales prices, hence the name of the method. The properties used for comparison are called comparables. Not just any properties work as comparisons, however. Properties are only considered comparables if they are very similar to the property and have been sold within the year under ordinary market conditions.

Overall, three or four comparables are used in this method. Obviously, no two comparables are exactly the same. So, how can this method be more accurate?

To account for differences in comparables, some adjustments are made to sales prices. These alterations are based on other factors that influence the rental property's market value. The most important of these factors is, you guessed, location. Location can significantly alter the sales prices of investment properties. Physical aspects of the property also come into play. Some of these include the square footage, the number of bedrooms and bathrooms, the condition, and the interior of the income property. The age of the property is also taken into consideration, as well as the market's conditions during the purchase. As a matter of fact, the purchase itself is analyzed, to see if the seller sold in a desperate attempt or sold to family.

2.) Cost Approach

The second approach from the main property valuation methods is the cost approach. The concept of the cost approach is that a real estate investor shouldn't buy a rental property for more than what it could cost to construct a replicate of said property. This approach uses one of the common property valuation methods, the sales comparison approach. The sales comparison approach is used to find the value of the property's land based on comparables. Then the costs of building the property are estimated, taking depreciation into consideration.

Another aspect that separates this method from other property valuation methods is what kind of real estate it is used for. The cost approach is not used for residential or income property real estate. It's used for properties that are usually constructed and not sold, like schools, religious institutions, government buildings, and hospitals.

Once the property's land value is estimated, it is summed with the estimated building costs of the real estate property. Building costs can be estimated in different ways. One common way includes finding out the cost of a square foot and multiplying it by the total square footage of the comparables.

After a sum of the building costs and land value is found, the depreciation costs are subtracted. There are three types of depreciation costs. The first is physical deterioration costs, which include deterioration that can be repaired, like old paint. The second type is functional obsolescence. This refers to aspects of the property that are not desirable in the present time. Examples include low ceiling and homes with one bathroom but multiple bedrooms. The third type of depreciation is economic obsolescence, or deterrents based off location, like being next to a loud airport.

3.) Income Capitalization Approach

The final approach of the property valuation methods is the income capitalization approach. This method is all for income properties. Apartment buildings, commercial real estate, and multifamily homes are examples that can be used in this approach. The income capitalization approach takes into account the return on investment and the net income of a property.

This method subdivides into two property valuation methods:

Direct capitalization focuses on a property's income. A property's annual gross income is estimated. The effective gross income is then estimated by considering the impact of vacancies. From there, the net operating income is calculated after subtracting expenses. The property's value is then estimated using the property's capitalization rate, or cap rate, and net operating income.

The second approach is through gross income multipliers. This method is used for real estate properties that are not initially purchased as income properties but end up being used as such. Examples include family homes. The monthly or annual gross income of the rental property is calculated. Then, the sales price of the property is divided by its rental income. This calculates the gross income multiplier, which is then used to find the property's market value.

Knowing the main property valuation methods is vital to for real estate appraisal. While landlords and investors do not necessarily have to know the ins and outs of the property valuation methods, it's always a good idea to have a basic idea.

VI.2 FACTORS CONSIDER IN VALUATION

Criteria vary for determining whether an existing appraisal or evaluation remains valid, depending upon the condition of the property and the marketplace and the nature of any subsequent transaction. The institution must document the information sources and analyses used for validation. Factors that could cause changes to originally reported values include:

I. The passage of time.

> ➢ Have any changes occurred in the marketplace or to the subject property since the original transaction date? Federal regulation does not establish time frames during which appraisals or evaluations are presumed to be valid. Volatility in the marketplace. Have any significant changes occurred since the original transaction? What is the effect of these changes on the subject property's market value?

II. The availability of financing.

> ➢ What are the current interest rates? How available is money to finance a real state transaction in the current market, compared to when the subject property transaction occurred?

III. The inventory of competing properties.

> Have there been any changes to supply-and-demand factors? What effect do they have on the occupancy potential of the subject property?

IV.   Improvements and physical changes.

> Have improvements been made to the subject property or to competing properties that could be viewed as negative influences on value? Has the subject property been properly maintained since the date of the previous appraisal? Is there deferred maintenance that could cause a loss in value?

V.   Zoning changes.

> Have there been any zoning changes? Could they dramatically affect the property's potential of continued development?

VI.   Environmental changes to the subject property.

> Has the property, its improvements, and the adjoining and surrounding properties been subject to any environmentally hazardous

changes since the previous appraisal? Examples of environmental changes may include the discovery of asbestos in the subject improvements and ground water contamination caused by leaks in underground storage tanks (USTs) on or near the subject site.

VII. **External obsolescence.**

➢ Does the property suffer from external changes since the previous appraisal? Examples include the closing of a school in the neighborhood, the construction of a penitentiary near the site, and the redevelopment of a major roadway to alleviate traffic congestion.

VI.3 What You Should Know About Real Estate Valuation

Estimating the value of real estate is necessary for a variety of endeavors, including financing, sales listing, investment analysis, property insurance and taxation. But for most people, determining the asking or purchase price of a piece of real property is the most useful application of real estate valuation.

Basic Valuation Concepts

a) Value

Technically speaking, a property's value is defined as the present worth of future benefits arising from the ownership of the property. Unlike many consumer goods that are quickly used, the benefits of real property are generally realized over a long period of time. Therefore, an estimate of a property's value must take into consideration economic and social trends, as well as governmental controls or regulations and environmental conditions that may influence the four elements of value:

- Demand: the desire or need for ownership supported by the financial means to satisfy the desire
- Utility: the ability to satisfy future owners' desires and needs
- Scarcity: the finite supply of competing properties
- Transferability: the ease with which ownership rights are transferred

b) *Value Versus Cost and Price*

Value is not necessarily equal to cost or price. Cost refers to actual expenditures – on materials, for example, or labor. Price, on the other hand, is the amount that someone pays for something. While cost and price can *affect* value, they do not *determine* value. The sales price of a house might be $150,000, but the value could be significantly higher or lower. For instance, if a new owner finds a serious flaw in the house, such as a faulty foundation, the value of the house could be lower than the price.

c) *Market Value*

An appraisal is an opinion or estimate regarding the value of a particular property as of a specific date. Appraisal reports are used by businesses, government agencies, individuals, investors and mortgage companies when making decisions regarding real estate transactions. The goal of an appraisal is to determine a property's market value – the most probable price that the property will bring in a competitive and open market.

Market price, the price at which a property actually sells, may not always represent the market value. For example, if a seller is under duress because of the threat of foreclosure, or if a private sale is held, the property may sell below its market value.

d) Appraisal Methods

An accurate appraisal depends on the methodical collection of data. Specific data, covering details regarding the particular property, and general data, pertaining to the nation, region, city and neighborhood wherein the property is located, are collected and analyzed to arrive at a value. Appraisals use three basic approaches to determine a property's value.

Direct Capitalization

Appraisers will perform the following steps when using the direct capitalization approach:

- Estimate the annual potential gross income.
- Take into consideration vacancy and rent collection losses to determine the effective gross income.
- Deduct annual operating expenses to calculate the annual net operating income.
- Estimate the price that a typical investor would pay for the income produced by the particular type and class of property. This is accomplished by estimating the rate of return, or capitalization rate.

- Apply the capitalization rate to the property's annual net operating income to form an estimate of the property's value.

Gross Income Multipliers

The gross income multiplier (GIM) method can be used to appraise other properties that are typically not purchased as income properties but that could be rented, such as one- and two-family homes. The GRM method relates the sales price of a property to its expected rental income. For residential properties, the gross monthly income is typically used; for commercial and industrial properties, the gross annual income would be used. The gross income multiplier method can be calculated as follows:

Sales Price ÷ Rental Income = Gross Income Multiplier

Recent sales and rental data from at least three similar properties can be used to establish an accurate GIM. The GIM can then be applied to the estimated fair market rental of the subject property to determine its market value, which can be calculated as follows:

Rental Income x GIM = Estimated Market Value

The Bottom Line

Accurate real estate valuation is important to mortgage lenders, investors, insurers and buyers and sellers of real property. While appraisals are generally performed by skilled professionals, anyone involved in a real transaction can benefit from gaining a basic understanding of the different methods of real estate valuation.

VI.4 How To Evaluate A Real Estate Developer?

Finalising a deal for a home should be a well-researched and thoughtful decision as you will be investing your hard-earned money into it. But, before you sign on the dotted line, you must evaluate the real estate developer on all the parameters. Howsoever difficult it may be, a thorough inspection will hold you in good stead in the long run.**Background check**

It is the most important point of evaluation. As a prospective customer, you should be aware of the name of the developer. His goodwill in the market, stability and active presence in the industry are matters of concern that you must focus on. Brand value is another factor that makes a developer standout.

Past projects and quality

The work of the developer will speak for its authenticity. Check the past projects delivered by him. A quality check of the past projects can also give an insight into the type of quality and project he will deliver at the time of possession.

Legal advice

Taking an opinion from a legal consultant can help you in making the final decision. A legal expert can help you check if the developer has all the necessary approvals and is following the building codes in his projects. The land where the project is coming up should be approved by the authority so as to avoid any future legal complications.

Financial position

It is important to check the financial position of a developer and how he manages his funds. His source of funds should not directly be affected by market sentiments. How he manages his funds can help you judge his success rate. Timely completion and delivery of his projects are also affected due to his financial position.

Reviews

Taking reviews from past customers can give you a better picture of the work of the developer. You can also refer to the customer feedback provided on several real estate websites. Ask buyers about the facilities and maintenance provided by the developer and the delivery time.

VI.5 Real Estate Evaluation and Analysis for Investors

Real Estate Investment Evaluation is Both Quantitative and Qualitative

I was taking a look at a potential investment the other day. It was a sprawling four unit multi-family property that was being occupied in its entirety the owner, who had been there for thirty years. The owner was an eclectic academic and there was every manner of bric-a-brac and antique scattered throughout the place. The place wasn't sub-divided properly. Carpet needed to be replaced and floors repaired. The shifting foundation had bulged the floor in places and had created large cracks that ran up and down various walls.

But how to evaluate a deal like this? Or any deal, for that matter? Personally, I break the considerations down into two categories:

• Quantitative: How do I expect the property to perform as an investment? For this part, I can whip out my calculator, or my spreadsheet, or my evaluation software and run some numbers.

• Qualitative: I have to ask myself "can I pull it off?" If you're like the vast majority of real estate investors, then you're a part-timer. That means you're going to have to tackle this project on top of your "day job" and manage it afterward. This part of the analysis will take some soul searching; a calculator isn't going to help you here.

A. Quantitative - Running the Numbers Using Cap Rate

Personally, I tend to look at three key figures when I'm considering an investment. Cap rate, is the first of these tools.

Cap rate is simply the annual net income divided by the price of the property. For years, investors have been using the "1% rule" which simply states that the monthly rental income for a property should be roughly 1% of the price that you pay for the property. Some markets have moved away from this ratio due to rocketing property values, but in others, you can still find properties that fit the 1% rule. Something that you should keep in mind, though, is that the 1% rule of thumb is a fair indicator of whether or not the property is going to generate enough cash flow on an annual basis to cover mortgage payments plus expenses. There, of course, are a lot of variables that go into this (from taxes to interest rates to the percent down payment that you pay) but it's a starting point.

B. Cash Flow as a Quantitative Evaluation Tool

The only reason you care about cap rate is that you're really trying for an easy proxy for what kind of cashflow the investment is going to generate. In investing, cash is king – ignore this calculation at your peril.

Estimating cashflow entails plotting out the major expected cash outflows (taxes, principal, interest, expenses, vacancies, fees, repairs) and comparing it with the income that the property produces. You can do this either via a spreadsheet or use a real estate evaluation software package.

C. Rate of Return as a Quantitative Real Estate Investment Analysis Tool

Cashflow, in turn, will allow you to calculate the property's expected rate of return (ROR). Rate of return is a measure of profitability; it measures the cash that a project will generate vs. the cash that you have to put into the project.

You'll need a spreadsheet or a real estate evaluation software to calculate this ratio. I think it's highly useful because it allows me to compare the return I'm expecting for the investment vs. the return I would reasonably expect for other, dissimilar investments. For example: if I ran the numbers for the property I described at the beginning of this article and it kicked back to me a rate of return of 8% I'd surely pass.

I can expect to get 8% investing on the stock market (lower risk, and a whole lot less effort). For the risk and effort I'd have to put into this project I'd expect a rate of return well north of 20%.

D. Qualitative - Can You Get the Project Done?

As I mentioned above, your calculator won't help here. This is when you need to take a look in the mirror and think about how much time and effort you're going to be able to devote to the project.

Again, let's look at the project I talked about at the start of this article. Let's say you're comparing it against a similar opportunity; another multi-family in the same neighborhood but which requires less work. You'd take that opportunity over the fixer-upper unless the second one offered a considerably higher rate of return. But how much higher?

To starting investors I always offer the same advice: In this area err on the side of caution. A project that you can get done is infinitely better than one that has you burned out by the time you're halfway through it. Find something in your comfort range that offers some decent numbers, get it done, then move on to a more challenging (and hopefully more profitable) project the next time around.

Conclusion:

Analysis is part art, part science.

VI.6 How to Enhance the Value of Your Property

The goal of any property investment is to increase the value; you want it to be worth more than when you bought it. There are low-cost ways to add value and there are more expensive and in-depth renovations that can be done. Here are 15 tips, both low and high cost, for increasing the value of your property.

a. Low-Cost Tips to Increase Property Value

There are simple things any property owner can do which can boost the appeal of your property. While these simple tips may not add tens of thousands of dollars to your property's value, without doing them, you may not be able to realize the full potential value of your property. These fixes can be done without having to hire any outside help. Although they are low cost, they can make a huge difference in the way your property looks.

1. **Clean:** Making sure your property is clean will have an immediate return on the value of your property. This includes both the outside and the inside. Garbage, dirt, and strange odors are not attractive features.
2. **Paint:** You will be amazed by the difference a fresh coat of paint can make. It can revive and brighten a tired space. Neutral colours are universally appealing.
3. **Add Curb Appeal:** A few strategically placed plants, a new mailbox, outdoor lights or shutters can make your property more inviting. Higher cost and potentially

higher return projects include new siding, new walkways, or driveways and adding a deck.

4. **Change Fixtures:** Changing out a doorknob, light switch cover, cabinet handle or even a light fixture is an easy way to breathe new life into a space.

5. **Stage the Property:** De-cluttering a space and giving each room a function can add value because many buyers lack imagination. Proper placement of furniture, the size of furniture, and amount of furniture is also key.

b. Moderate/High-Cost Tips to Increase Property Value

There are updates you can make to a property that can have an average to high cost depending on the extent of the renovation done and the materials chosen. These types of updates have the potential to add significant value to your property.

1. **Add Architectural Detail:** You can give a boring room some character by adding a chair or crown molding to it.

2. **Change/Add Windows or Doors:** This is a valuable addition. Not only does it improve the aesthetics of the home, it also can reduce noise inside the home, help

lower heating bills and cooling bills and increase natural light inside the home. French doors that lead out to the backyard add elegance, open up the space, and allow more light to enter the property. Skylights can also help brighten up spaces that may be lacking windows or natural light. Properly positioning windows and doors can also help highlight a beautiful view that your property may have or minimize one that is not so desirable, such as a brick wall or a view right into your neighbor's home.

3. **Change Flooring:** Updating carpet or adding hardwood or tile adds value to a property.

4. **Reduce Noise:** People want to feel like their home is an oasis. There are many ways to reduce noise such as adding insulation, installing double pane windows and doors, installing carpets and rugs to minimize footsteps and placing plants to further absorb noise.

5. **Update a Kitchen or Bath:** This includes changing a portion of the room, but not an entire gut renovation. It could be changing the flooring or changing countertops. In the bathroom, you could switch out a toilet, sink or bathtub. In a kitchen, it could include buying new appliances.

6. **Gut Renovate a Kitchen or Bath:** This would be a complete overhaul of the room. It can involve adding

new cabinets, new countertops, new flooring, new lighting fixtures, new appliances, new sinks, new faucets, new cabinet handles, new tub, new shower, new toilet or even changing the layout of the room.

7. **Update Siding:** There are many options for home siding and the best type will often depend on the climate and area where your property is located. It is an update that will improve the aesthetic look of your property and can help lower your utility bills.

8. **Create a More Functional Layout/Modernize Floor Plan:** For example, it could be taking down a wall between a kitchen and living room. It could be rearranging a kitchen to create more usable space. It could be adding a bathroom to the master bedroom to create a suite. It could also be swapping the location of two rooms, such as an office and a dining room to create a better flow in the home. It could also be taking space away from one room to add it to another room, for example, taking some space from an oversized living room to create a pantry for the kitchen.

9. **Add More Square Footage:** This does not only mean adding an addition to the property. It could also mean finishing an unfinished attic or a basement to add more living space to the property. It could also mean

transforming an attached garage into additional living space.

10. **Gut Renovate a Property:** Completely redoing a property by ripping it down to its studs and building it back up with a more modern design and materials can increase the value of a property, as long as you are able to sell the property for more than you owe on the property along with renovation and holding costs.

c. Do Not Over-Improve

While you want to improve your property and increase the value, you also want to be cautious so that you do not over-improve your property. You don't want to spend an amount of money on a renovation where you will not see a return on your investment. For example, putting high-end Viking appliances in a home in a middle-class neighbourhood would be an over-improvement.

Before you renovate, do some research on your area to find out how much the property will be worth after the renovations, otherwise known as the After-Repair-Value or ARV. Once you properly gauge this new value, you can deduct the price you paid for the home and what you are left with is the maximum price you should spend for the renovation and any soft costs such as financing charges, closing costs, and holding costs if the property will sit vacant while the renovations occur.

VI.7Things That Can Cause Property Value to Decrease

As an informed property investor, you should be aware of the value of your property at all times. Certain things can cause the market price to decrease. Some of these things, such as natural disasters, are out of your control. Here are three threats to your property's value.

- **Increasing Mortgage Rates, Decreasing Property Value**

When mortgage interest rates are low, buyers can afford to spend more on a house. At lower interest rates, their monthly mortgage payments will be lower and they will pay less over the life of the loan.

As interest rates increase, home affordability decreases for potential buyers. They can't afford to spend as much on the initial purchase price because, with the increased interest rates, their monthly mortgage payments will be higher and they will have to pay more over the life of the loan.

Mortgage rate increases not only affect home buyers, but they affect sellers as well. Your home is not as valuable because people have to pay more to buy your home at the higher rates. Before the interest rates rose, your home may have been in the price range of 30 prospective buyers. With the higher rates, this number may have decreased to only 10 prospective buyers.

You may have a harder time selling your home at the current list price. You may have to **drop your list price** in order to appeal to more buyers.

- **Weather Decreases Home Value**

Mother Nature can cause a decrease in your property's value. I'm not talking about the occasional heavy rainstorm or three feet of snow. I'm referring to natural disasters that can wipe out entire communities. Examples of natural disasters that can threaten your property's value are hurricanes, tornadoes, wildfires, earthquakes, tsunamis, mudslides and floods.

Weather patterns can also change over time. When you bought your home, it may not have required flood insurance. One hurricane could come in and cause flooding in your town. The flood zone maps would then be altered and require you to have flood insurance. This requirement will significantly impact the value of your home as people will be hesitant about buying property in a flood zone.

Natural disasters will damage your existing property. If you have insurance, you will usually get some money to pay for the damage, but it is rarely enough . You can apply for aid from FEMA, but it is usually hit or miss with whether you will qualify for their aid and how much they will give you. Sometimes these storms completely destroy a property and it is not salvageable.

Not only do you have to worry about repairing the damage caused by these storms, if your property is still standing, you have to worry about ever being able to sell your property. People will be very apprehensive about buying property in an area that was just devastated by a disaster.

- **Foreclosures/Short Sales Decrease Neighbourhood Value**

Another threat to the value of your property are foreclosures and short sales in your neighbourhood. These affect your property value by skewing the comparable sales in your neighbourhood down.

VII.COMMERCIAL LEASE

A lease is a contract outlining the terms under which one party agrees to rent property owned by another party. It guarantees the lessee, also known as the tenant, use of an asset and guarantees the lessor, the property owner or landlord, regular payments from the lessee for a specified number of months or years. Both the lessee and the lessor face consequences if they fail to uphold the terms of the contract.

VII.1 Commercial Real Estate Lease Types

Finding a landlord and tenant match in commercial real estate requires a commercial real estate lease type that benefits both. The needs of the landlord are income from rent and the control of costs to assure a profit. The tenant wants to peg their rental costs as closely as possible also. Using the right type of lease, they can both satisfy their needs with a bit of negotiation at times.

1. ## The Gross Lease

    a) The gross lease in commercial real estate is sometimes described separately from the full service lease. However, the difference is not great, and most people consider them together. Learn how they are the same, the difference and how the gross commercial lease differs from other commercial real estate lease types.

2. ## The Triple Net Lease

    The triple net lease in commercial real estate requires that the tenant pay a significant share of expenses of operation, as well as all taxes and insurance related to their rental unit. This type of lease helps the landlord by fixing their costs, as their rents are fixed. Tenants aren't fond of this type of lease especially in older properties.

3. The Modified Net Lease

As a compromise between the gross leaseand the triple net, the modified net lease is quite helpful in helping landlords and tenants to structure lease terms that work for both. This article gives the details of how they differ from the other lease types.

4. The Percentage Lease

A Percentage Lease is a lease that typically requires a tenant pay "Base Rent" and then on top of that amount pay a percentage based on monthly sales volumes. Percentage leases are commonly executed in retail mall outlets but depending upon the location and nature of the business can have a dramatic impact on percentage rent.

If You Want to Practice in Commercial, Know these Well

When a residential real estate agent sees the fat commissions involved with commercial real estate transactions, the lure is strong. Why not move over to commercial and enjoy the high life? I agree that I'd rather be getting high five and six figure commissions rather than the average residential check. But, it's not a cake walk getting there. Often a commercial deal can take many months or more than a year to get from initial interest to the closing table. For the new agent, we then need to add sometimes a year or more before they actually build a sphere of influence that will get them a buyer or seller client. So, if you have an interest in commercial real estate, by all means see if you can live the dream. But, put a plan together to make personal expenses when you may not see a commission for a while.

The Gross Lease in Commercial Real Estate

Though some sources break out the full-service lease type from the gross lease in commercial real estate, they are more often the same. The landlord pays for:

- Taxes

- Insurance
- Maintenance

The gross commercial lease is used most often in multi-tenant and single tenant office buildings, industrial and some retail properties. The landlord collects fixed rents and pays the expenses out of them.

As costs increase over time, many gross and full-service leases will contain escalation clauses that increase rents over time to offset tax increases and higher insurance and maintenance costs. It is important that a tenant shopping for space understand any escalation clauses to project rent expense into the future.

The gross lease works well for office tenants and some retail properties. For many retail properties, especially those with seasonal income fluctuations, the percentage lease is better. This allows their rent to fluctuate with income.

Other Types of Commercial Leases

Let's take a quick overview look at other commercial lease types:

Triple Net Lease: The triple net lease is used extensively in commercial real estate. It is popular for multi-tenant industrial and retail properties. With tenants whose expenses vary greatly, such as an industrial user of electricity, the triple net lease is best for the landlord.

Modified Net Lease: The modified net lease is a compromise between the gross lease and the triple net. The landlord and tenant usually set up a split of maintenance expenses, while the tenant agrees to pay taxes and insurance. Utilities would likely also be negotiated in the modified net lease.

Percentage Lease: A Percentage Lease is a lease that typically requires a tenant pay "Base Rent" and then on top of that amount pay a percentage based on monthly sales volumes. Percentage leases are commonly executed in retail mall outlets but depending on the location and nature of your business can have a dramatic impact on percentage rent.

The Modified Net Lease in Commercial Real Estate

The modified net lease is a compromise between the gross lease and the triple net. The landlord and tenant usually set up a split of maintenance expenses, while the tenant agrees to pay taxes and insurance. Utilities would likely also be negotiated in the modified net lease.

This type of lease might be used in industrial, retail or multi-tenant office properties. Tenant resistance to triple net leases, especially in older properties, makes the modified net lease more popular. It allows a compromise situation that shares the costs of building operation and maintenance.

The terms of a modified net lease are as varied as are building and tenant business types. The flexibility of this lease type makes for easier agreement between tenant and landlord. Many a lease has been put together because of creative modified net lease terms.

Why is this Lease Type Popular?

To answer that question, let's think about the many varied uses for commercial lease space. Business requires profit to continue to exist (unlike government). The business owner spends much time and effort in analyzing their revenues and expenses, as well as their product or service pricing to manage that necessary profit.

- **Clothing store:** This business owner is concerned about lighting and displays, and that lighting is a major consumer of electricity. Possibly the landlord would want to negotiate utilities with the business. While there is a seasonal component to clothing, the inventory is just adjusted for the season. So, this business owner may want to negotiate a lease that is fixed in amount each month, but share in repair expenses, as there isn't much in the way of repairs in a clothing store space.

- **Light Manufacturing or Assembly:** Often the equipment in these businesses belongs to the business, not the landlord, so repairs and maintenance would fall on the tenant. However, depending on the electricity or gas consumption of the equipment, there may be some negotiation of utilities.
- **Usage Risk Considerations:** Suppose a building has historically been used as a warehouse and the new tenant is going to do some light manufacturing or component assembly. If this changes the insurance hazard profile for the structure, the insurance would go up, and the landlord would likely want to take care of that with a negotiated modified net lease arrangement.

The Triple Net Lease in Commercial Real Estate

The triple net lease is used extensively in commercial real estate. It is popular for multi-tenant industrial and retail properties. With tenants whose expenses vary greatly, such as an industrial user of electricity, the triple net lease is best for the landlord. In the triple net lease, many of the expenses of operating the property are passed along to the tenant.

The landlord gets the advantage of not having to foot the bill for tenants who are wasteful of utilities or rough on their spaces, requiring more maintenance and repairs. The tenants must be more careful and watch their expenses. In older and less efficient structures, the tenants are footing ongoing expenses that are higher because the building hasn't been renovated and needs some work.

VIII.   REAL ESTATE AGREEMENT

An agreement refers to negotiated and usually legally enforceable understanding between two or more legally competent parties.

Although a binding contract can (and often does) result from an agreement, an agreement typically documents the give-and-take of a negotiated settlement and a contract specifies the minimum acceptable standard of performance

VIII.1Contract Conditions

When you formally make an offer on a home you want to buy; you'll fill out a lot of paperwork specifying the terms of your offer. Aside from the obvious things like the address and purchase price of the property on which you're making an offer, here are some items you should be sure to include in your real estate purchase contract.

1. Finance Terms

If you are like most people and you won't be able to buy the home without obtaining a mortgage, your purchase offer should state that your offer is contingent upon obtaining financing at a specified interest rate. It is beneficial that you research interest rates in advance and try to get pre-approved for a mortgage.

If you are paying all cash for the property, you should state this as well because it makes your offer more attractive to sellers. Why? If you don't have to get a mortgage, the deal is more likely to go through, and closing is more likely to happen on time.

2. Who Pays Specific Closing Costs

The agreement should specify whether the buyer or seller will pay for each of the common fees associated with the home purchase, such as escrow fees, title search fees, title insurance, notary fees, recording fees, transfer tax and so on. Your real estate agent can advise you as to whether it is the buyer or seller who customarily pays each of these fees in your area.

3. Home Inspection

Unless you are buying a tear-down, you should include a home inspection contingency in your offer. This clause allows you to walk away from the deal if a home inspection reveals significant and/or expensive-to-repair flaws in the structure's condition.

4. Fixtures and Appliances

If you want the refrigerator, dishwasher, stove, oven, washing machine or any other fixtures and appliances, do not rely on a verbal agreement with the seller and do not assume anything. Specify in the contract any fixtures and appliances that are to be included in the purchase.

VIII.2 Real Estate Listing Agreements Types: Who Gets Paid and Who Doesn't

To avoid lawsuits, state laws require home sellers to make it clear to which agents, and the terms under which, they will pay commission. However, sellers need not worry about how to make their wishes known. Real estate agents are trained in the rules of representation and are required by law to explain all listing options to their seller-clients. They also provide the correct legal-and-binding forms and enter the information in their local multiple listing service databases so that all agents who wish to show homes know exactly whether and how they'll be paid when the listing goes live.

A. Open Listing

An open listing is the type most used by homes For Sale by Owner, or FSBOs. The owners retain the right to sell the property themselves and pay no commission to anyone. However, **many owner-sellers are willing to pay a commission to the real estate agent who brings them a qualified buyer**. FSBO sellers usually indicate that they are willing to pay commission in their classified ads or on their yard signs with words such as "brokers welcome" or "brokers protected." Such offers to pay commission are not guaranteed by open listing agreements, though, and savvy agents execute written commission agreements with FSBO sellers before showing such properties to their clients.

B. Exclusive Agency Listing

In this type of listing, FSBO sellers execute an agreement with one real estate brokerage firm and agree to pay that broker a commission **only if its agent is the** procuring cause **of the sale**. No other brokers are invited to bring buyers. The sellers retain the right to search for buyers simultaneously, and they don't owe the broker any commission if they are successful in their efforts.

C. Exclusive Right to Sell Listing

This type of listing **provides the greatest commission protection for the listing** real estate broker. The property sellers agree to pay the listing broker a commission no matter who brings the buyer, including the owners themselves. A broker with an exclusive-right-to-sell agreement is protected and more willing to invest in getting her client's home sold.

D. What Agents Need to Know

In aggressively representing their buyers, particularly in markets with low inventory, real estate agents might be out looking for any properties available. Knowing the type of listing agreement the sellers have with their agent saves a buyer's agent time and potential lost earnings -- after all, there's not much an agent can do if she shows her clients a home they love but the seller won't pay commission. For this reason, agents should study listings closely before agreeing to show them to their clients and take steps to protect any potential commission up front.

The good news is that exclusive-right-to-sell listings make up the the vast majority of multiple listing service properties for sale. In such cases, the seller signs a listing agreement to pay 100 percent of the commission to the listing broker should their property sell during the listing period, and the listing broker agrees to share a portion of the commission to the broker who brings a buyer.

VIII.3 Duties and Responsibilities of Real Estate Broker

A real estate broker is a person licensed to negotiate and arrange real estate transactions. It would include writing contracts for listing and purchasing homes, land, and commercial properties. The broker is a higher level license than a real estate agent and would be authorized to hire real estate agents to work under the broker's supervision.

There can be a considerable risk if agents are not properly trained and supervised, particularly with regards to fair housing and environmental regulations. Brokers who allow agents to make major mistakes can end up sharing in the penalties, both financial and legal.

When it comes to agents having their own websites, it is good practice for their supervising broker to check them from time to time to make sure there are no violations of regulations.

What Real Estate Brokers Do

I'm going to break this into three sections, one for how they work with real estate sellers, another for buyers, and the third for their duties and responsibilities in supervising agents under their license.

- **Brokers working for sellers:** While many times an agent working on a broker's behalf will take on these duties, the broker often handles transactions for sellers as well. Some of their duties on behalf of sellers include:
  - Share the listing commission with successful buyer brokers.

- Advise the home seller in preparing their home for listing and showings.
- Supervise showing, report to sellers results and feedback.
- Submit any and all offers to the seller for consideration.
- Help the seller to negotiate offers to try and execute a purchase contract with a buyer.
- Work on the seller's behalf in coordinating the transaction process.
- Deliver and explain documents, disclosures and transaction items.
- Work with the seller through to the closing and their move-out from the home.

- **Brokers working with Buyers:** This is the other side, working with people wanting to buy a property with advice and services to help them to locate the property and complete the transaction.
    - Help buyers to locate all properties in their desired area in their price range and meeting their criteria.
    - Coordinate and help buyers to visit and view properties.

- When a decision is made to attempt a purchase, help the buyer to craft their initial offer and purchase agreement.
- Work with the buyer on their behalf in negotiations with the seller through their agent/broker.
- Once a purchase contract is executed, coordinate the transaction process on the buyer side.
- Deliver and explain documents in the transaction process.
- Coordinate inspections, reports and repair negotiations.
- Assist buyers through to closing and taking possession.

- **Supervising Agents:** When a broker is licensed to have agents working under them, sometimes called a supervising or managing broker, their agents handle most or all of the brokerage transactions. With the supervision of agents the broker:
  - Verifies continued licensing of all brokerage agents.
  - Instructs and trains or provides training resources for agents.

- Is responsible for agent behavior, performance, and legal compliance.
- Provides some services and marketing resources for agents.
- Often maintains a brokerage website for agent marketing.

Real estate brokers licensed at the highest state levels set the standards of practice in the area and are tasked with maintaining high levels of customer/client service and compliance with all state real estate laws.

VIII.5How RERA making impact on real estate Industry?

With an objective to protect consumer interest and to bring efficiency and transparency into the country's real estate sector, the Government of India implemented the RERA Act nationwide on May 1 this year.

The RERA Act is aimed at addressing the grievances of property buyers who at times are cheated by developers on delay in delivery of under-construction properties, execution of said project plans, legitimacy of properties, etc., and is being touted as pro-consumer law.

The pre-RERA position

Prior to the Act, it has been a well settled position under law that the lenders were entitled to enforce security over land and recover their outstanding debt, without reference to the purchasers who had also acquired rights in the unit being built on the land.

For self-owned property of the promoter, the lender was also empowered to take over the management of the borrower, or the project and cause the project to be completed.

Even secured creditors and notified NBFCs under the Securitisation and Reconstruction of Financial Assets and Enforcement of Security Interest Act, 2002 ("**SARFAESI**") could take recourse under SARFAESI which included the sale of the charged property (whether land or development rights) without the intervention of the court.

Mortgage of development rights on the other hand would typically require the consent of the society members/ landowner, unless specifically permitted in the development agreements in favour of the promoter/ developer.

This is in view of the fact that development rights are in the nature of license to enter upon and construct which are personal in nature and usually extended to the developer on the basis of the repute of the specific developer and cannot be said to have created a right in rem at large.

Establishment of the regulatory authority: The absence of a proper regulator (like the Securities Exchange Board of India for the capital markets) in the real estate sector, was long felt. The Act establishes Real Estate Regulatory Authority in each state and union territory.

Its functions include protection of the interests of the stakeholders, accumulating data at a designated repository and creating a robust grievance redressal system.

To prevent time lags, the authority has been mandated to dispose applications within a maximum period of 60 days; and the same may be extended only if a reason is recorded for the delay.

Further, the Real Estate Appellate Authority (REAT) shall be the appropriate forum for appeals.

Compulsory registration:

According to the central act, every real estate project (where the total area to be developed exceeds 500 sqmtrs or more than 8 apartments is proposed to be developed in any phase), must be registered with its respective state's RERA.

Existing projects where the completion certificate (CC) or occupancy certificate (OC) has not been issued, are also required to comply with the registration requirements under the Act.

While applying for registration, promoters are required to provide detailed information on the project e.g. land status, details of the promoter, approvals, schedule of completion, etc. Only when registration is completed and other approvals (construction related) are in place, can the project be marketed.

Reserve account: One of the primary reasons for delay of projects was that funds collected from one project, would invariably be diverted to fund new, different projects.

To prevent such a diversion, promoters are now required to park 70% of all project receivables into a separate reserve account. The proceeds of such account can only be used towards land and construction expenses and will be required to be certified by a professional.

Title representation: Promoters are now required to make a positive warranty on his right title and interest on the land, which can be used later against him by the home buyer, should any title defect be discovered.

Additionally, they are required to obtain insurance against the title and construction of the projects, proceeds of which shall go to the allottee upon execution of the agreement of sale.

Standardisation of sale agreement: The Act prescribes a standard model sale agreement to be entered into between promoters and homebuyers. Typically, promoters insert punitive clauses against home buyers which penalised them for any default while similar defaults by the promoter attracted negligible or no penalty.

Such penal clauses could well be a thing of the past and home buyers can look forward to more balanced agreements in the future.

Penalty: To ensure that violation of the Act is not taken lightly, stiff monetary penalty (up to 10% of the project cost) and imprisonment has been prescribed against violators.

Here are 10 key benefits of RERA Act for home buyers:

1. All real estate developers/promoters have to compulsorily register ongoing and upcoming real estate projects with RERA

2. Home buyers will have to pay only for carpet area

3. Developers/promoters will have to disclose project related details, including: project plan, layout, and government approvals related information to the customers such as sanctioned floor space index (FSI), number of buildings and wings, number of floors in each building, etc.,

4. Developers/promoters will have to transfer 70% of the money received from buyers for particular project to an escrow account. These funds should be used only to cover the cost of construction and land cost

5. The real estate act includes projects that are ongoing on the date of commencement of the Act that is May 1, 2017 and for which the completion certificate (CC) has not been issued.

6. Developers/promoters have to register their projects with RERA before advertising or marketing

7. RERA 2016 recommends imprisonment for a term which may extend up to three years, or fine which may extend up to 10% of the estimated cost of the real estate project, or both, in case of non-compliance with the Act

8. If any developer/promoter provides false information or contravenes the provisions of registration of real estate projects - has to pay penalty upto 5% of the estimated cost of the project

9. Developers/promoters have to update project details quarterly on the RERA website

10. Any structural defect, or any other obligations of the developer/promoter as per the agreement for sale, brought to notice of developer/promoter within five years from possession to be rectified free of cost

What RERA means for Consumers, Developers and Others:

However, with the impending rules for its implementation and setting up of the RERA Authority in several States, its execution remains to be tested. To add to this, what the optimists fail to notice, is how RERA regime is neither a novel concept, given the existing framework governing the sector in most States, nor does it provide a fool-proof method for resolution, transparency, accountability and efficiency.

Impact of RERA on real estate industry

- Initial backlog.
- Increased project cost.
- Tight liquidity.
- Rise in cost of capital.
- Consolidation.
- Increase in project launch time.

Initially, a lot of work is to be done to get the existing and new project registered. Details such as status of each project executed in last 5 years, promoter details, detailed execution plans, etc., needs to be prepared.

With the advent of RERA, specialised forums such as the State Real Estate Regulatory Authority and the Real Estate Appellate Tribunal, will be established for the resolution of disputes pertaining to home buying and the aggrieved party will have no recourse to other consumer forums and civil courts, on such matters. While the RERA sets the groundwork for fast-tracking dispute resolution, the litmus test for its success, will depend on the timely setting up of these new dispute resolution bodies and how these disputes are resolved expeditiously with a degree of finality.

IX. REAL ESTATE AGENT

An agent is any person who has been legally empowered to act on behalf of another person. Agents are employed to represent their client in negotiations or dealings with third parties.

Real estate agents are licensed professionals who negotiate and arrange the buying and selling in real estate transactions. Most agents work for a real estate broker or realtor who has additional training and extra certifications. Agents usually work completely on commission, so their income depends on their ability to assist clients and close transactions.

IX.1 Referral Fees in Real Estate Brokerage

Definition: Referral fees in the real estate business are fees charged by one agent or broker to another for a client referred. They are most common when a seller client is leaving the area and their agent refers them to an agent or broker in the new area to which they're moving. Generally this fee is a percentage of the final commission received by the agent who accepts the referral.

That's how free markets work, or they should.

Am I about to go on a rant that real estate agent referrals aren't of value to the customer/client? Not really, but with some commentary. I personally do not ever request a referral for advising a customer or client to contact a specific broker or agent. I will only do so if I know the agent/broker personally and know how they do business. That limits my referrals to a local level, which means it doesn't happen often.

Real estate referral fees are fees paid when one agent or broker refers a client to another agent or broker based on the eventual commission when the sale closes. While real estate referral fees range from 20% to 35%, the standard fee is about 25% of the earned commission. You must be a licensed real estate agent or broker to be paid a commission fee.

The 4 Basic Steps to Referring your Real Estate Client

If you are fortunate to have the ability to refer an existing client to an agent that you trust, and have never done so before, the general procedure is straightforward.

Step 1: Standardize Your Referral Contract

While most brokerages have forms that agents use in their real estate referral fee agreements, we wanted to provide a form that can be customized for your use. Every referral contract should at least include the agent and broker licensure on both sides of the transaction, the duration of contract, and specifics of the agreed upon referral fee as a percentage.

The first element of any real estate referral agreement is to include names, addresses, and license information for both the referring agent/brokerage and the receiving one. Everyone should be clear in their ability to confirm the identity, location, and licensure of both the agents and companies on each side of the transaction.

Step 2: Get Client Approval

Meeting with your client is an important part of gathering referral information, and addressing any client concerns or questions. Your client is the most essential element of the referral process. Not only must they be using the referred realtor for you to receive your fee, but you want to be sure you do them a genuine good to preserve your reputation in the industry. Be sure that you have all the details of where and when they are relocating, how soon they anticipate purchase, their financial status in the process (are they already qualified for a mortgage?), what they will be looking for, and how serious they are about purchase.

Step 3: Make the Referral

At the time you contact your referral agent, you should have all the details to make the process go smoothly and quickly. You will have the mentorship of your broker to know what to expect, the timeline and information from your client to give the agent a solid heads-up, and a form that will likely contain all of the information of both parties along with your standard real estate referral fee that is ready for signature. If you don't already have another agent to refer your client to, there are services that will help you find one which we discuss in more detail below.

Step 4: Negotiate the Fee

With most real estate referral fees, the standard 25% is both expected and well-received, but sometimes there may be room for you to negotiate this upward if your broker allows it. For example, you might increase your referral fee ask to 30% if you have a client who is already qualified for a mortgage, has already sold his previous residence, is making a larger purchase, and will likely be buying in the next month.

X. TYPES OF PROPERTIES&

LOANS

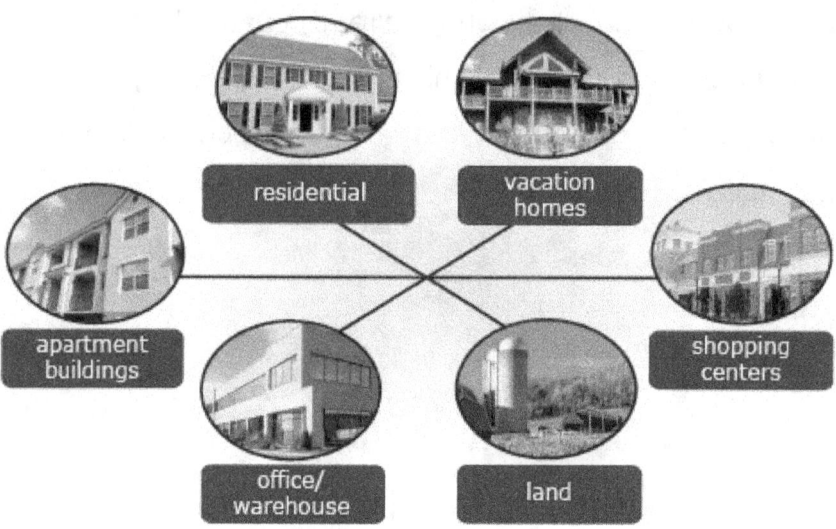

X.1 Types of Investment Properties

"Investment properties" refers to income-producing properties or properties that can readily be flipped for a profit. Primary residences which see returns in the form of capital appreciation are not included here.

- **The Single Family Investment Property**

The single-family investment property is a house or condominium bought with the intention of renting or selling it to a single tenant or buyer. Common ways to invest in single-family properties include buying foreclosures, fixer uppers or other properties believed to be undervalued for the area. The main goal is to buy something you feel is undervalued, fix it up and sell it for a quick profit, or rent it out to a single tenant or family. You should believe that the ARV is much greater than the purchase price.

Pros:

- They are smaller properties, so they require a smaller investment.

Cons:

- When the economy is bad, it will be harder to flip a property because fewer people are able to buy.
- A vacancy in a single family home or condo means you will have zero returns until you are able to find a tenant.

- **The Second Home/Vacation Home Investment Property**

The second home or vacation home becomes a rental property when the homeowner decides to rent it out when they are not there.

An example would be a family who owns a beachfront condo in Miami that they only use from December to February. The other nine months out of the year, they look for tenants to rent the condo from them. It doesn't matter if they rent it to one person for the whole nine months or 25 different people within the nine month period. As long as they are receiving rental income, it is considered an investment property.

Pros:

- You may not have considered renting out your vacation home, so any rental income is just passive income in your pocket.

Cons:

- A vacancy in a single family home or condo means you will have zero returns until you are able to find a tenant.

- o It will be harder to rent a beach front home in the northeast in the dead of winter or a ski-lodge in the heart of summer.

- **The Small Multifamily Investment Property**

This is a two- to four-unit house or building. The small multifamily is the most common type of investment property for beginners. It can be an owner occupied property or all units can be occupied by tenants.

Pros:

- Offers stable returns. There is always demand for apartments regardless of the economy.

Cons:

- You are responsible for the property maintenance and operating costs of the building.
- Tenant leases are short, typically one year, so there may be a lot of turnover.
- With so few units, vacancies, especially prolonged vacancies, will have a large impact on your return.

- **The Large Multifamily Investment Property**

This investment property is made up of five or more residential units. Apartment complexes fall under this category. This type of property can also be owner occupied (although not as common) or all units can be occupied by tenants.

Pros:

- Offers stable returns. There is always demand for apartments regardless of the economy.
- Having a vacancy in this type of property will not impact your profit as much as the loss of a tenant in a single family home or retail property for example.

Cons:

- You are responsible for the maintenance and operating costs of the building.
- Tenant leases are often short, about a year, so there may be a lot of turnover.

- **The Mixed Use Investment Property**

A mixed use property is a property that is used for a combination of residential and commercial purposes. This type of property is often seen in urban areas.

For example, it can include a combination of apartments and stores, such as a three family with a Laundromat on the first floor and two apartments above it. It could also be a combination of offices and apartments, for example, a 25 unit building with a real estate office on the ground floor and apartments above it.

Pros:

- o The commercial property has a supply of customers from the tenants above and the tenants have convenient access to the retail below, such as a deli.
- o You will receive two streams of income, one from the residential part and one from the commercial part.

Cons:

- It is harder to get financing for mixed-use properties because they are seen as riskier investments because it is, in essence, two separate businesses that are trying to succeed.
- Construction costs are higher than for single-use properties.

- **The Office Investment Property**

This can include one tenant (a company) or multiple units (offices) for multiple tenants (companies).

Pros:

- You can get considerable rent from office tenants.

Cons:

- Often require a large investment, as offices are often located in downtown areas.
- If you have a vacancy, it will be much harder on your pocketbook.
- Office buildings offer variable returns as employment is directly tied to the strength of the economy.

- **The Retail Investment Property**

Again, this could be one tenant, such as a small ice cream parlour or a large store like a Wal-Mart, or it can include multiple units for multiple tenants, such as a strip mall with a nail salon, pizza parlour and drug store, or a power center with over 250,000 square feet of space.

Pros:

- ○ Retailers tend to sign long leases which can give you stability.

Cons:

- ○ Their success is generally tied to how healthy the economy is.

X.2 Types of Commercial Real Estate Construction Loans

Developers and investors who purchase underutilized land or run-down properties have special needs due to the financing that is required to get their properties up to speed.

Not only must these clients worry about selling, occupying or owning a project, but they must obtain specific financing to make the land, and any buildings on it, habitable.

We're talking about projects that can range from a few thousand dollars to hundreds of millions of dollars in construction financing needs. Often a developer will have or locate funding to buy the land outright, then use the land as full or partial collateral for the remaining funds needed.

Commercial development can be very risky, and getting funding can be tricky if the developer and others involved do not have a track record of successful projects. Sometimes the developers are the owners upon completion and can use other properties they have developed as collateral if there is enough equity in them. These are some of the most common types of construction loans.

❖ Land Development Loan

When raw or undeveloped land needs to be made construction-ready a land development loan can be obtained. The raw land may be subdivided and sold as a number of parcels for commercial or residential use. It may also include the installation of sewer, water or power lines to the site.

❖ Acquisition and Development Loan

An A&D loan is appropriate if raw land is ready to be developed, or is already developed but needs improvements to its infrastructure or existing buildings. The A&D loan usually covers both the purchase of this land and the cost of any improvements needed before the development can be completed.

❖ Mini Perm Loan

This is a temporary loan typically used to settle an outstanding construction or commercial property loan on a project that, once completed, would produce income. After three to five years of generating income, the mini-perm loan is replaced with long-term financing. Mini-perm loans are normally obtained through commercial banks.

❖ Takeout Loan

A takeout loan can provide permanent financing on projects where a temporary loan, such as a short-term construction loan, currently exists. Many lenders require their developers to secure a takeout loan before a short-term loan can be granted.

Paras Mittal

❖ Interim Construction Loan

This pays for the labor and materials used to construct a project. An interim construction loan is usually valid for 18 to 36 months and is settled once a long-term mortgage is in place.

It's a New World With Crowd funding

This is a whole new ballgame for commercial project financing. Crowd funding brings together many smaller investors to pool funds for specific projects. Doing a Google search on "crowd funding" yields a number of companies engaged in the business. They make their money on fees paid by both the investors and the developers.

There are still hurdles for most wannabe small investors. Though things are loosening up a bit, most of these opportunities are open only to "Accredited Investors." Federal Regulations govern who is considered accredited, and there are several qualifying situations, mostly related to net worth and investment knowledge.

The good news is that crowd funding is growing rapidly and the government is beginning to open up ways for smaller investors without significant net worth to get involved. It's becoming mainstream, and projects from small office buildings and supermarkets to high rise condominiums are being funded this way. If you want to brag about owning a piece of the new huge shopping mall in your city, this is the way you may be able to make it happen.

Existing Commercial Real Estate

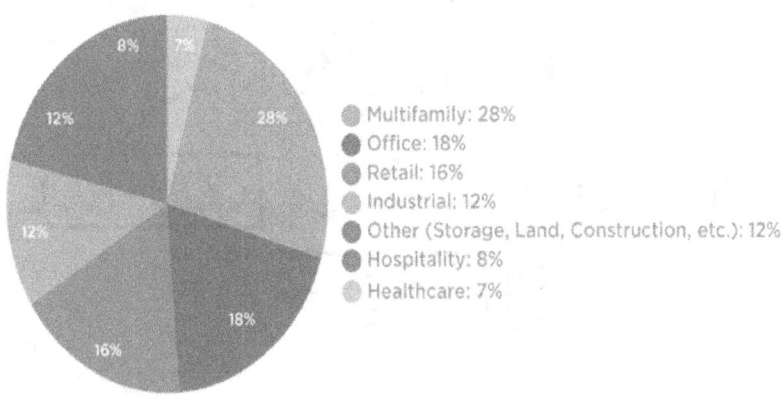

Multifamily: 28%
Office: 18%
Retail: 16%
Industrial: 12%
Other (Storage, Land, Construction, etc.): 12%
Hospitality: 8%
Healthcare: 7%

XI. RISK MANAGEMENT

Nature of Risk Risk Management and Real Estate Risk is a critical factor in commercial real estate. Risk is a complex topic and comes in many forms, making it difficult to identify much less quantify and manage.

Thus, it is useful to start with a simple definition and then add some of the complexity to the equation. In a pragmatic sense, risk can be defined rather simply as the –Difference between expectations and realizations.

‖ That is, it is a measure of the uncertainty surrounding a current or future event or state of nature. It is the uncertainty that something will not be as it seem today, or that some prediction or assumption about what will occur in the future turns out to be wrong.

Risk in inherent in real estate due to its temporal nature: uncertainty is inherent in anything marked with the passage of time.

Real estate risk is more complicated than other asset classes due to the:

1) inefficiency, behavioral nature and dual Space-Time, Money-Time dimensions of the market, and

2) the capital-intensive, durable and vulnerable nature of individual assets to external forces. These external forces make real estate vulnerable to unknown forces that can create windfalls (i.e., unexpectedly high returns) or wipeouts

XI.1 Risk management in Real Estate Property Management

Administration and risk management is a critical component of real estate property management. The record-keeping function must be carefully managed and, the greater the level of detail, the better the likely results.

In most states, by far the greatest number of consumer complaints, commission penalties and license suspensions and revocations are related to property management. It's not that those licensees doing property management are dumb. It's that it is a very transaction intensive business. While an average agent might do a dozen sale transactions a year with a purchase agreement and related documents, the average property manager might do hundreds of smaller transactions.

The fact that they're smaller doesn't make those transactions less important and it doesn't reduce the risk involved in doing them. As a property manager, you're contracting with an owner to market and rent their property, collect the rents and remit them to the owner, and to manage the property, from maintenance to tenant rules enforcement.

In doing this, you're transacting with owners, tenants, repair companies, advertising media, contractors, and others. Each and every one of these transactions introduces some risk into your business. It's not necessarily a lot of risk in each case, but it is cumulative.

The financial functions are by far the most likely to create problems for the broker. Financial functions involve:

- the marketing & financial function requires records of expenditures and income, as well as tax records, advertising invoices and more,
- tenant management involves records of all their requests, rental payment history and rules violations, and
- facility maintenance & repairs require maintenance schedules, repair records for warranty, and employee and subcontractor personnel records.

The risk management component is of course very important. A large disaster can threaten the survival of the property economically. The records kept are a part of this, as any legal action taken by others can be thwarted if there are detailed records that refute their claims.

A part of risk management is a determination of risk versus reward. A good example is a hot tub or swimming pool on the property. The property manager and owner must balance the value of the pool with the risks incurred. When a risk such as this is identified, there are three ways in which it can be addressed:

1. **Avoidance** - The decision can be made to remove the hot tub or pool, as the additional rental income is not worth the cost of insurance or the risks involved.

2. **Control** - If the hot tub is retained, perhaps a coded lock and fence would be installed to keep out younger children.

3. **Risk Transfer** - The most prevalent way of dealing with risk is to purchase insurance to transfer the risk to the insurer.

The successful property manager will plan for problems, keep excellent files and records of every activity, and continually assess these functions to determine if a change is necessary.

Documents and Email

In many states, you're only required to maintain transaction records for six years. However, it is advisable to keep them longer, especially if you're allowed to do so in electronic format. You can bet that if any of the parties may have a claim, someone who wants to sue you for something six years and ten days ago will still have their document copies. It's much more difficult to plead your case if you've already destroyed your copies.

When it comes to email, any court action involving a federally guaranteed loan (pretty much all of our residential deals), can compel you to produce emails related to the transaction and communications with your customer/client. There are numerous ways and software products to save related emails, but read some of the articles here about Evernote, a solution for many reasons. Here's how to handle email using Evernote and your Gmail archives. Modify to fit your email solution.

- Set up automatic forwarding in Gmail of every email to or from your customer/client.
- They go into a notebook in Evernote for the transaction.
- A couple of weeks after closing, pull up all of those emails in Evernote and print them in chronological order to a PDF file.

THANK YOU

Author contact details are as follows:

Paras Mittal (ACA,ACS,NCFM)

Legal firm web site: www.pnjlegal.com

Facebook Profile: https://www.facebook.com/paras.mittal.75

Twitter Profile: https://twitter.com/parascs

Linked In Profile: https://www.linkedin.com/in/paras-mittal-1645377 Mb: India +91-8506916129

Disclaimer:

judgments, facts, and recitals on public domain. We reserve rights to allow credits to any particular person or body for the reference taken from his personal viewpoints. You should consult your own Investment, Real estate, tax, legal and accounting advisors before engaging in any transaction.

www.ingramcontent.com/pod-product-compliance
Lightning Source LLC
Chambersburg PA
CBHW081513220526
45467CB00010B/2895